D0879408

New York State Coach, Empire Edition, English Language Arts, Grade 4

Coach™

Triumph Learning®

New York State Coach, Empire Edition, English Language Arts, Grade 4
288NY
ISBN 10: 1-60471-738-6
ISBN 13: 978-1-60471-738-9

Cover Image: The New York City skyline with the New York countryside. Illustration by John Patrick/Deborah Wolfe Ltd.

Triumph Learning® 136 Madison Avenue, 7th Floor, New York, NY 10016

Printed in the United States of America.

10 9 8 7 6 5 4 3

Table of Contents

Letter to the Student

Dear Student,

Welcome to *Coach*! This book provides instruction and practice with all the important skills you need to know, and gives you practice answering the kinds of questions you will see on your state's test.

The *Coach* book is organized into chapters and lessons, and includes a Pretest and Posttest. Before you begin the first chapter, your teacher may want you to take the Pretest which will help you identify skill areas that need improvement. Once you and your teacher have identified those skills, you can select the corresponding skills lessons and start with those. Or, you can begin with the first chapter of the book and work through to the end.

Each of the lessons has three parts. The first part walks you through the skill so you know just what it is and what it means. The second part gives you a model, or example, with hints to help your thinking about the skill. And the third part of the lesson gives you practice with the skill to see how well you understand it.

After you have finished all the lessons in the book, you can take the Posttest to see how much you've improved. And even if you did well on the Pretest, you'll probably do better on the Posttest because practice makes perfect!

We wish you lots of success this year, and hope the *Coach* has been a part of it!

Test-Taking Checklist

Here are some tips to keep in mind when taking a test. Take a deep breath. You'll be fine!

✓ Read the directions carefully. Make sure you understand what they are asking.

✓ Do you understand the question? If not, skip it and come back to it later.

✓ Reword tricky questions. How else can the question be asked?

✓ Try to answer the question before you read the answer choices. Then pick the answer that is the most like yours.

✓ Look for words that are **bolded**, *italicized*, or underlined. They are important.

✓ Always look for the main idea when you read. This will help you answer the questions.

✓ Pay attention to pictures, charts, and graphs. Do you understand the information? Sometimes they can give you hints.

✓ If you are allowed, use scrap paper. Take notes and make sketches if you need to.

✓ Always read all the answer choices first. Then go back and pick the best answer for the question.

✓ Be careful marking your answers. Make sure your marks are clear.

✓ Double-check your answer sheet. Did you fill in the right bubbles?

✓ Read over your answers to check for mistakes. But only change your answer if you're sure it's wrong. Your first answer is usually right.

✓ Work at your own pace. Don't go too fast, but don't go too slow either. You don't want to run out of time.

Good Luck!

New York State English Language Arts Performance Indicators

Performance Indicator	Description	Lesson Correlation
READING		
Standard 1: Students will read, write, listen, and speak for information and understanding.		
R.1.b	Collect and interpret data, facts, and ideas from unfamiliar texts	1
R.1.c	Understand written directions and procedures	6
R.1.d	Locate information in a text that is needed to solve a problem	1, 3, 4
R.1.e	Identify a main idea and supporting details in informational texts	2
R.1.f	Recognize and use organizational features, such as table of contents, indexes, page numbers, and chapter headings/subheadings, to locate information	7
R.1.h	Identify a conclusion that summarizes the main idea	2, 5, 11
R.1.k	Use text features, such as headings, captions, and titles, to understand and interpret informational texts, with assistance	7, 8
R.1.l	Use graphic organizers to record significant details from informational texts	9
Standard 2: Students will read, write, listen, and speak for literary response and expression.		
R.2.e	Explain the difference between fact and fiction	18
R.2.f	Make predictions, draw conclusions, and make inferences about events and characters	11, 12
R.2.i	Use specific evidence from stories to identify themes; describe characters, their actions, and their motivations; relate a sequence of events	13, 14, 16
R.2.j	Use knowledge of story structure, story elements, and key vocabulary to interpret stories	13, 14, 15, 16
R.2.p	Use graphic organizers to record significant details about characters and events in stories	9

Performance Indicator	Description	Lesson Correlation
READING (continued)		
Standard 3: Students will read, write, listen, and speak for critical analysis and evaluation.		
R.3.a	Evaluate the content by identifying - the author's purpose - whether events, actions, characters, and/or settings are realistic - important and unimportant details - statements of fact, opinion, and exaggeration, with assistance - recurring themes across works in print and media	16, 17, 18, 19, 20
Applicable Core Performance Indicator		
R.CPI.11	Determine the meaning of unfamiliar words by using context clues, dictionaries, and other classroom resources	10
LISTENING AND WRITING		
LW	Listening/Writing Cluster	21, 22, 23, 24, 25, 26, 27
RW	Reading/Writing Cluster	23, 24, 25, 26, 27
WM	Writing Mechanics Cluster	28, 29, 30, 31, 32

CHAPTER

Information and Understanding

1 Locating Information

R.1.b, R.1.d

Getting the Idea

A **detail** is a piece of information. There are many types of details. Names and descriptions are details. Actions and events are also details. When you read, you will be asked to find and remember important details.

Every passage contains details. Let's take a look at some of the different types of details you should look for.

Examples of Details
names of places and characters
dates and times
description of the environment
things that characters say and do
things that the narrator tells you
facts in an article

What is the best way to find details when you are answering a question? First, try to remember what you read in the passage. If you can remember what you read, you will probably be able to find details easily. You should always check the passage before you give your answer. This will help make sure that your answer is correct.

If you cannot remember where you saw the answer, use the "skim and scan" method. To do this, quickly look through the story or article without reading every word. Scan the sentences, looking for an important word that will tell you that you are looking in the right place.

For example, if you were looking for the name of a character's pet hamster, you would start at the beginning and scan the selection, looking for the word *hamster*.

Coached Example

DIRECTIONS
Read this passage and answer the questions that follow.

Annika loved to play the piano. As a child, she used to listen to her mother play. When she was a teenager, playing the piano became second nature to her. She liked the way the keys felt under her fingers. The sound the instrument made always made her smile. She could almost feel the music around her. She hoped that one day she would be a great pianist, like Mozart.

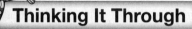

Thinking It Through

1. What first inspired Annika to play piano?

   A. Mozart

   B. her mother's playing

   C. her sister's playing

   D. the way the keys felt

   HINT Look through the passage for a key word such as *child*. Then read the surrounding words and sentences to find the answer.

2. What always made Annika smile?

   A. the way the keys felt

   B. stories about Mozart

   C. any type of music

   D. the sound the piano made

   HINT The answer to this question is clearly stated in the passage. The best way to find a detail is to skim and scan. You know that if you look for the word *smile*, you will find the answer quickly.

Lesson Practice

Coached Reading

DIRECTIONS
Read the passage below. While you are reading, look to the Reading Guide for tips.

Koalas

1   Koalas are found only in Australia. Koalas are marsupials. This means they carry their babies in a pouch. Koalas are not bears, even though people sometimes call them "koala bears."

2   The name *koala* means "no drink." Koalas do not drink water very often. They get the water they need from their food.

3   Koalas eat almost nothing but eucalyptus leaves. These leaves are poison to most animals, but not to koalas. Even though koalas eat only one type of food, they are still picky eaters. They sniff each leaf until they find one they will eat.

4   Koalas spend most of their time sleeping in trees. They sleep during the day and eat at night. Koalas prefer to live alone. Usually, koalas are almost silent. During mating season, though, the males can make quite a loud call.

5   Koalas are rather small marsupials. They stand about two feet tall and weigh about thirty pounds. They curl into a furry ball when they sleep. These animals have round ears with long hair. Koalas have thick woolly fur that is gray on their back and white on their front. Their paws have five claws, with two claws acting like thumbs. This helps them climb and hang onto trees.

Reading Guide

Why don't Koalas drink very often?

Where do Koalas sleep? When do they eat?

Independent Practice

DIRECTIONS
Use the passage to answer questions 1–5.

1. What do koalas eat?

    A. insects

    B. eucalyptus leaves

    C. apples

    D. small animals

2. When do koalas eat?

    A. at all times of day and night

    B. during the day

    C. at night

    D. only in the morning

3. What is a marsupial?

    A. a kind of kangaroo

    B. an animal with a pouch

    C. an animal that eats plants

    D. a kind of bear

4. Where do koalas sleep?

    A. in nests on the ground

    B. in trees

    C. under rocks

    D. in caves

5. Why do koalas rarely drink water?

    _____

    _____

    _____

2 Main Idea and Supporting Details

R.1.e, R.1.h

Getting the Idea

How would you answer the question, *What is this passage about?* Would you make a list of everything that a passage talks about? Would you read every word in the passage to the person who asked? No. Instead, you would tell the person the main idea of the passage. The **main idea** tells what a passage is mostly about.

Let's practice finding the main idea. Read the passage below, and think about what it is mostly about.

> The first living thing from Earth to go into outer space was a dog. The dog, Laika, blasted off in 1957. The Soviet Union launched Laika into space. The next year, two mice from the United States went up into space. In 1963, France sent a cat named Feliette up on a rocket. In 1969, a chimp named Ham flew into orbit.

What is the main idea of this passage? The main idea is *Many different animals have been sent into space.* To figure out the main idea of an article, think about the main thing you learn from reading it. The main idea can sum up the whole passage.

The other sentences in the passage support the main idea. They give **details**, or information, that tell more about the main idea. This web can help you picture how the main idea and details in a passage work together.

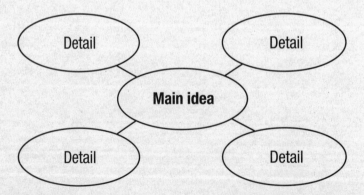

Coached Example

Read this passage and answer the questions that follow.

Building a model railroad is a fun hobby. Many people enjoy it. A model railroad is a copy of a real one. But it is much smaller.

A model railroad can have lots of parts. It must have trains and tracks. It might also have signals, switches, bridges, or stations. Some people build whole little towns. All the parts can be bought already made. Some people would rather buy kits. Then they can build the parts.

Model trains are not the same as toy trains. A model train tries to copy a real train. Toy trains do not have the fine details of model trains. Another way they are different is in scale. Scale is the size of something compared to the real thing. Model trains are usually smaller than toy trains.

A model railroad also uses electric power. People wire the tracks. Then the trains can really run. It is fun to run your own tiny railroad!

Thinking It Through

1. What is the main idea of this passage?

   A. Model trains look like real trains.

   B. Model railroads are a popular hobby.

   C. Some people buy kits.

   D. Toy trains do not have fine details.

   HINT A main idea can sum up the whole passage. Only one answer talks about the whole passage. The others are details.

2. What is the main idea of the second paragraph?

   A. A model railroad may have many parts.

   B. Some people build whole little towns for the model railroads.

   C. Any of the parts can be bought already made.

   D. Some people would rather buy kits than build their own railroads.

   HINT Think about what the paragraph is mainly about. Look back at the paragraph to see which sentence states the main idea and which sentences give details.

Lesson Practice

Coached Reading

DIRECTIONS

Read the passage below. While you are reading, look to the Reading Guide for tips.

Strawberry Alarm Clock

Reading Guide

1   A lot of rock and roll bands have odd names. In the 1960s, there was a group called the Electric Prunes. Another band was called the Guess Who. One of the strangest band names was Strawberry Alarm Clock.

> A lot of bands do have odd names. Is there more in the paragraph about this? Is this the main idea of the paragraph?

2   Strawberry Alarm Clock was a band from California. In 1967, they had a hit song called "Incense and Peppermints." It sold over a million copies. Radio stations all over the country played it. The group was very famous for a while.

3   The funny thing is that the man who sang this song was not a member of the band! The singer was a teenager named Greg Munford. He was hanging out with the band the day they were recording the song. For fun, he got up and sang the song while the band played.

4   Even though this song became very popular, Greg never joined the band. He had his own band, but they never had a hit.

5   Strawberry Alarm Clock had a few more hits. None of their songs was as popular as "Incense and Peppermints." The band finally broke up in 1971.

> Strawberry Alarm Clock had one big hit. What main idea does this detail support?

Independent Practice

DIRECTIONS
Use the passage to answer questions 1–4.

1. What is the main idea of paragraph 1?

    A. A lot of rock bands have odd names.

    B. In the 1960s, there was a group called the Electric Prunes.

    C. Another band was called the Guess Who.

    D. One of the Strangest band names was Strawberry Alarm Clock.

2. Which detail gives information about the band Strawberry Alarm Clock?

    A. Strawberry Alarm Clock had a few more hits.

    B. Greg had his own band.

    C. Greg's band never had a hit.

    D. One band was called the Guess Who.

3. What is the main idea of the entire passage?

    A. Strawberry Alarm Clock was a band that was popular for a short time.

    B. Strawberry Alarm Clock is an odd name.

    C. Greg Munford sang a hit song for the band.

    D. Strawberry Alarm Clock's biggest hit was "Incense and Peppermints."

4. What is the main idea of paragraph 3?

    _____

    _____

    _____

3 Cause and Effect

R.1.d

Getting the Idea

What would happen if you hit your finger with a hammer? You would probably feel pain and yell, "Ow!" This is an example of cause and effect. **Cause** is the reason that something happens. **Effect** is what happens. In this case, hitting your finger with the hammer is the cause. Feeling pain and yelling are the effect.

Most of the passages you read include causes and effects. Figuring out the cause and effect will help you understand the passages. Let's take a look at some examples of cause and effect.

Cause	Effect
Tom throws a baseball at the house.	A window gets broken.
Noela says she likes Wilma.	They become friends.
The baby hears a loud clap of thunder.	The baby gets frightened.

The event that happens in the box on the left results in the event that happens in the box on the right. One cause can have many effects, and one effect can have many causes.

Cause and effect questions can work both ways. You may be asked why something happened, or what the cause was. You could also be asked what happened after something else happened, or what the effect was. To figure out cause, ask yourself *why* the effect happened. To figure out effect, ask yourself *what* happened after the cause occurred.

Coached Example

Read this passage and answer the questions that follow.

A camera is a device used to take photographs. The word *camera* comes from Latin. It means "dark chamber." A camera is like a dark box. You use it to copy an image.

There are many kinds of cameras. In general, a camera needs light and film that can react to light. First, you point the camera at the subject you want in the picture. Then you press a button that lets light into the camera. Light bounces off the subject and goes into the camera through a lens. The light passes through the lens and then makes an upside-down picture of the subject on the film.

To take good pictures, it is important to let in the right amount of light. If too much light hits the film, the picture will look washed out. If not enough light hits the film, the subject will be hard to see against the background. Two things affect how much light gets into the camera. One is how fast the camera opens to let in the light. The other is how big the opening is.

Thinking It Through

1. What happens when light passes through the lens of a camera?

   A. You press a button that lets light into the camera.

   B. Light bounces off the subject.

   C. The light makes an upside-down picture on the film.

   D. The camera opens quickly to let in light.

   HINT   This is a *what* question. It asks for an effect. Look back to find out what happens when light passes through the lens.

2. Why would a picture look washed out?

   A. Too much light hits the film.

   B. Light bounces off the subject.

   C. The light makes an upside-down picture on the film.

   D. Not enough light hits the film.

   HINT   This is a *why* question. It asks for a cause. Look back in the passage to find out what causes a picture to look washed out.

Lesson Practice

Coached Reading

DIRECTIONS
Read the passage below. While you are reading, look to the
Reading Guide for tips.

Spring Peepers

Reading Guide

1   Spring peepers are small frogs that live in the eastern
part of the United States. They all have dark "X"s on
their backs. Sometimes the marking is not clear, so it can
be hard to see, but it is there.

Why is the mark hard to see? Look for a cause.

2   Spring peepers are mostly nocturnal. Because they
are small and are active at night, people do not often
see spring peepers. They do hear them, however. Early
spring is the start of mating time for spring peepers. The
males use a very loud, peeping call to find mates. This
call gives the spring peeper its name.

Why do peepers peep? Look for a cause for the sound they make.

3   Besides trees, spring peepers need water in their
habitat, or home area. Usually, spring peepers live in
woods near marshes, ponds, or streams. They mate in the
water. They also lay their eggs there.

4   In their egg and tadpole form, spring peepers are food
for fish, water insects, turtles, and other animals in the
water. As adults, spring peepers are prey for bullfrogs,
snakes, and skunks. Spring peepers eat small insects such
as flies, ants, and small spiders.

5   When it gets very cold, spring peepers hibernate.
This means they go to sleep for a while, and their body
functions slow down. They hibernate under logs or in
loose bark on trees.

What do the frogs do because of the cold? Look for an effect.

Independent Practice

DIRECTIONS
Use the passage to answer questions 1–5.

1. Why is the "X" on the peeper's back sometimes hard to see?

   A. The frog is dark-colored.

   B. The marking is not always clear.

   C. The marking is not always there.

   D. People are not out at night.

2. What causes peepers to peep?

   A. It is mating time.

   B. It is getting cold.

   C. It is feeding time.

   D. It is hunting time.

3. What effect does cold have on spring peepers?

   A. It causes them to die.

   B. It causes them to peep.

   C. It causes them to hibernate.

   D. It causes them to climb trees.

4. Why do spring peepers live near water?

   A. They drink a lot of water.

   B. They mate and lay eggs in water.

   C. They hide in the water.

   D. They eat mostly water bugs.

5. Why do people not see spring peepers very often?

   _____

   _____

   _____

   _____

4 Compare and Contrast

R.1.d

Getting the Idea

One way of understanding something is by looking at it next to something else. When you **compare**, you find the qualities two items share. When you **contrast**, you do just the opposite. You find the ways in which two things differ. The books you read for school, and the selections you read for class, will sometimes use the compare-and-contrast method. You need to watch for it and understand how it works.

Read the following passage, and think about how the topics compare and contrast.

> When you're choosing a pet, you have a lot to think about. Many people choose dogs or goldfish. In some ways, they are alike. Both dogs and goldfish need a lot of care. Each needs special food, made just for them. They can both be a lot of fun to watch. Puppies, though, need things to chew on. They also need to be walked outside each day. As you know, you can't walk a goldfish. A goldfish needs an aquarium. Puppies just need room to play.

One easy way to compare topics like these is to draw a Venn diagram. A **Venn diagram** is a graphic that shows how things are alike and how they are different. Here is an example using the passage you just read.

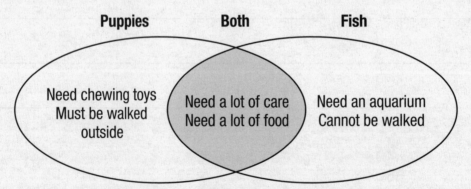

Coached Example

DIRECTIONS
Read this passage and answer the questions that follow.

After defeating their father, the three sons of Cronos divided up the universe. Zeus was the god of the thunder, and he carried a thunderbolt. He ruled the heavens and enforced justice on Earth. He had a goddess wife, Hera.

Hades was a grim and severe god. He almost never left his kingdom of the underworld, or his wife, Persephone. Persephone had not become queen of the underworld by choice. Hades had tricked her. One of Hades' important objects was a helmet of invisibility.

The ruler of the seas was Poseidon. He was an ill-tempered god. He could choose to help or harm sailors. Poseidon could also cause earthquakes. His weapon was the trident, a pole with three sharp prongs.

Thinking It Through

1. Which of the following is a similarity among Zeus, Hades, and Poseidon?

   A. They were all grim.

   B. They were all sons of Cronos.

   C. They all ruled the Earth.

   D. They all cared about justice.

   HINT Look back at the passage. Only Hades is described as grim. Only Zeus ruled Earth or was involved with justice.

2. Which of the following is a difference between Zeus and Hades?

   A. Zeus was a god, but Hades was not.

   B. Zeus's father was Cronos, but Hades' father was Poseidon.

   C. Zeus was not married, but Hades was.

   D. Zeus moved between the heavens and Earth, while Hades stayed in one place.

   HINT Carefully read the paragraphs about Zeus and Hades. You will be able to find the difference between them.

Lesson Practice

Coached Reading

DIRECTIONS
Read the passage below. While you are reading, look to the
Reading Guide for tips.

Are All Elephants the Same?

Reading
Guide

1   Do you think all elephants are pretty much alike?
They are big gray animals with trunks, right? Well, that
much is true about all elephants. All elephants are not
alike, though. There are two different kinds: African
elephants and Asian elephants.

2   Size is a noticeable trait. All elephants are large. In
fact, elephants are the largest animals on land. African
elephants, however, are larger than Asian elephants.
Their ears are larger than those of Asian elephants, too.
Some people say that the ears of the African elephant are
shaped like the continent of Africa.

What is the contrast here?

3   Elephants' trunks help make them unique. The trunk
is both the nose and upper lip of the elephant. Both
African and Asian elephants can pick up things with their
trunks. The trunk of the African elephant acts like two
fingers to grasp things; the trunk of the Asian elephant
acts like one finger. African elephants can pick up more
with their trunks than Asian elephants can. Elephants
also use their trunks to help them drink by drawing
water into their trunks, then pouring the water into
their mouths.

Is the author comparing
or contrasting?

4   Both types of elephant have tusks. In the Asian
elephant, though, only males have tusks you can see.
Both female and male African elephants have visible
tusks. Both African elephants and Asian elephants have
been hunted for their tusks.

What comparison is being
made about tusks?

Independent Practice

DIRECTIONS
Use the passage to answer questions 1–4.

1. What is a similarity between African elephants and Asian elephants?

   A. They both have ears shaped like Africa.

   B. They both have tusks.

   C. They both have trunks that act like two fingers.

   D. They both use their trunks like straws when they drink.

2. Which of the following sentences shows a contrast?

   A. All elephants are not alike.

   B. Both kinds of elephants have tusks.

   C. Only male Asian elephants have visible tusks.

   D. Male Asian elephants have visible tusks; female Asian elephants do not.

3. Which word shows a comparison?

   A. are

   B. both

   C. different

   D. however

4. Which sentence contrasts the two types of elephants?

   A. African elephants are larger than Asian elephants.

   B. Asian elephants have been hunted for their tusks.

   C. African elephants are gray.

   D. Asian elephants are nice.

5 Summarize

Getting the Idea

One way to help yourself understand what you read is to **summarize** what the author has written. A summary is a short way of stating the main ideas and important details in an article or story.

For example, read this paragraph.

Clouds and Weather

It is fun to watch clouds in the sky move and change shape and size. Did you know that you see different kinds of clouds in different weather? On a fair-weather day, you might see big puffy clouds. They might look like great puffs of cotton. They are called *cumulus* clouds. Cumulus clouds may change into *thunderheads*. Then they look long, dark, and flat at the top. Of course, they show that a thunderstorm is on the way. On a fair-weather day, you might also see wispy clouds that look like feathers. They are called *cirrus* clouds. On a cloudy day or rainy day, you would see *stratus* clouds. These clouds are flat.

Here is a summary of the article you just read.

There are different types of clouds that tell about different types of weather.

When you read, try to summarize what the author has written. Look for the main ideas and important details. Not all details should be included, though. Sometimes, the hardest part of writing a summary is deciding which details to leave out.

Coached Example

DIRECTIONS
Read this passage and answer the questions that follow.

Americans throw out tons of garbage every day. There are several ways of dealing with so much garbage. One way is to recycle things.

Recycling means making new things from old things. People can separate their garbage for recycling. Glass can be recycled. Old glass will become new glass. Things made of metal can be recycled, too. Old metal will then become new metal.

Another way to deal with garbage is to reuse items. If everyone threw away less, there would be less garbage to deal with. Empty jars and boxes can be reused to store things. Old newspapers can be reused for wrapping or doing arts-and-crafts projects.

Garbage can also be reduced. People make piles of garbage smaller by burning them to ash. Garbage is burned in ovens called incinerators. The ashes are then buried. Reducing garbage saves room in landfills.

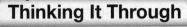

Thinking It Through

1. What would be a good title for this passage?

   A. America: A Giant Dump?

   B. Dealing with Garbage

   C. Recycling Is Best

   D. Ways to Reuse Trash

   HINT Remember that the title usually tells what the article is about. Only one of the titles deals with the whole article. The other titles each have to do with just one part.

2. Which is the BEST summary of the passage?

   A. Garbage can be recycled, reused, or reduced.

   B. We can reuse empty jars and boxes to store things.

   C. Old glass becomes new glass when it is recycled.

   D. Recycling means turning old things into new things we can use.

   HINT Remember that a summary is a short way of stating the main points of an article. The answer you choose must address all of the article—not just one idea.

Lesson Practice

Coached Reading

DIRECTIONS
Read the passage below. While you are reading, look to the Reading Guide for tips.

The "Poor Man's Milkshake"

Reading **Guide**

1   My grandma likes to talk about the way things used to be in the city. She remembers kids playing stickball in the streets outside their buildings and buying handfuls of candy for one penny.

2   Egg creams, though, are what she misses the most. What, you may ask, is an egg cream? An egg cream is a drink that's a lot like a milkshake, but without the ice cream. Egg creams were called poor man's milkshakes because they tasted like milkshakes, but they did not cost as much. An egg cream has neither eggs nor cream.

> What is the main idea of this paragraph?

3   People disagree about the origin of the first egg cream. Some think it began in Manhattan. Others say the Bronx was the true birthplace.

4   How do you make an egg cream? Take a very tall glass, and add a little chocolate or vanilla syrup to the bottom. Follow that with a few splashes of milk. Finally, add a spurt of plain seltzer water to make the milk nice and frothy.

> Are these details important to the meaning of the article?

5   Many restaurants have started making egg creams again. This means kids like me can get a taste of the old days.

Independent Practice

DIRECTIONS
Use the passage to answer questions 1–5.

1. What is the main idea of paragraph 1?

   A. The narrator's grandmother likes to talk about growing up in the city.

   B. The narrator's grandmother doesn't like the city.

   C. The narrator's grandmother likes watching stickball.

   D. The narrator's grandmother grew up in the city.

2. What is the main idea of paragraph 2?

   A. Egg creams do not contain eggs.

   B. Cream is not used to make an egg cream.

   C. Egg creams and milkshakes taste alike but are not the same.

   D. There is no ice cream in an egg cream.

3. What is the main idea of paragraph 3?

   A. People like egg creams.

   B. No one is sure where egg creams were invented.

   C. Egg creams are very common.

   D. Egg creams are good for you.

4. Which of the following is NOT an important detail?

   A. My grandma misses egg creams.

   B. Egg creams are made with syrup, milk, and seltzer.

   C. People disagree about where egg creams were created.

   D. Egg creams are coming back in style.

5. Write a summary of "The Poor Man's Milkshake" on the lines below.

   _____

   _____

   _____

1 Review

Directions
Read this article. Then answer questions 1 through 6.

The Erie Canal

by Bruce S. McCullough

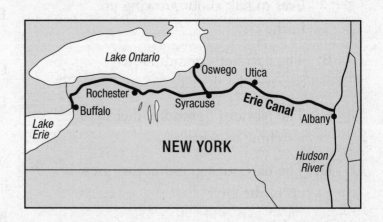

In the early 1800s, people in the United States needed to find a cheap way to move things between the east and the west. The big, useful rivers all ran north-south. The Appalachian Mountains were too difficult to travel across with heavy loads. Many people thought a waterway, or canal, should be built. The canal would run between Lake Erie and the Hudson River in the state of New York. This canal would allow boats to carry many tons of goods from one place to another. Horses and wagons could not match that.

Many plans were talked about. Finally, in 1817, the digging began. Few people knew the hard task facing the canal's builders. The final plan called for the canal to be 363 miles long, 40 feet wide, and 4 feet deep. A ten-foot wide path along the bank would allow large animals such as horses or mules to tow the boats. The entire canal would cross land that rose and fell almost 700 feet.

The builders had to deal with swamps and rivers. Bridges had to be built across the canal for roads and farms that were split in two by the waterway. For ten or more hours of hard work, the workers were paid about 80 cents a day.

The Erie Canal was finished in 1825. A series of locks could raise or lower the water level in parts of the canal. The locks let boats slowly climb the hilly areas and then go down the other side. The canal became the link between the Great Lakes to the west and the Atlantic Ocean in the east. It cost seven million dollars to build, but it greatly reduced shipping costs.

Before long, thousands of boats, horses, and people were at work moving goods on the canal. The low cost of shipping goods by water helped farmers settle on the rich lands of the Midwest. These farmers could then send their crops back to eastern markets. In return, they received finished goods. Later, the canal was improved by making it wider and deeper. Larger boats were able to use the canal and carry much bigger loads.

The Erie Canal was a great success for many years. But times and needs change. Little by little, railroads, trucks, and airplanes took over the job of carrying goods. Today, however, the canal is still being used. Bike paths and walking trails line its sides, and the water is used for pleasure boating.

1 In the article, what happened **right after** the Erie Canal was finished?

   A Bike paths and walking trails were put along its sides.

   B Railroads, trucks, and airplanes became more popular.

   C The canal was improved by making it wider and deeper for boats.

   D More farmers moved into the Midwest because of the lower costs.

2 What is this passage **mostly** about?

   A the series of locks along the Erie Canal

   B the need for and building of the Erie Canal

   C the importance of shipping in the United States

   D the changes in methods of shipping through history

Go On

3 Which sentence from the article **best** tells why a canal was needed to ship things by water between the east and the west?

A "The big, useful rivers all ran north-south."

B "The canal would run between Lake Erie and the Hudson River in the state of New York."

C "A ten-foot wide path along the bank would allow large animals such as horses or mules to tow the boats."

D "The entire canal would cross land that rose and fell almost 700 feet."

4 A series of locks were placed in the Erie Canal because they

A greatly reduced shipping costs

B allowed boats to get over hilly areas

C allowed large ships to pass through

D connected roads that were split in two

5 According to the article, what is **one** problem the canal's builders faced?

A They needed workers to dig 12 hours a day.

B They could not build the canal across farms.

C They had to deal with swamps in the canal's path.

D They had to build a path inside the canal for animals.

6 After reading the article, what could the reader conclude?

A It was a mistake to build the Erie Canal.

B The Erie Canal turned out to be a great success.

C The Erie Canal helped more merchants than farmers.

D It cost more to build the canal then it saved in shipping.

Directions

Read this article. Then answer questions 7 through 12.

Play Ball!

by Erin Naughton

Baseball is one of the most popular sports in the world. But where did it come from? A lot of people believe that it was invented in Cooperstown, New York, by a man named Abner Doubleday. Some experts think this is incorrect.

The story says that Doubleday invented the game in 1839. However, the word "baseball" has been around a lot longer than that. A letter from a minister in 1700 mentions the game. A book written in 1774 includes a short poem about baseball. The truth is that the game had been evolving for centuries before people started calling it "baseball."

The game of baseball most likely came from an old game called "rounders." The game of rounders was played on a diamond with a base in each corner, just like baseball. It also involved throwing and hitting a ball. A "striker" was a person who held a bat and tried to hit the ball. If he missed, it was a "strike." When he hit it, he would try to run around the bases without getting tagged. If he did not hit the ball after three swings, he was "out." This game is similar to baseball.

Why do people think that Doubleday invented the game? The story came from a man named Charles Spaulding. He made and sold sporting goods. He hoped people would buy more of his goods if they thought that the game was created in this country. He and some friends made up the story about Abner Doubleday. Then they spread the word. People heard the story so many times that they figured it was true. Spaulding's clever plan had worked!

Go On

No matter how it got its start, the game has become an American symbol. As far back as the 1870s, American sportswriters were calling the sport "The National Pastime" or "The National Game." Even if baseball came from Europe, Joe DiMaggio, Babe Ruth, and Lou Gehrig were all as American as they come. Also, the rules for baseball were standardized in the United States. These rules are now the official rules that are used when professional baseball is played in places like Japan, Australia, Mexico, and Puerto Rico. So, is baseball American or not? You be the judge.

7 According to the article, which statement about baseball is **true**?

   A It is only popular in America.

   B It was not mentioned before 1839.

   C It has become an American symbol.

   D It was invented by Charles Spaulding.

8 How are the games of rounders and baseball alike?

   A They both have a pitcher that throws balls.

   B They both have nine innings in each game.

   C They both allow players to slide to get onto bases.

   D They both require players to hit a ball before running.

9 Charles Spaulding made up the story that Abner Doubleday invented baseball because he wanted

   A to make more money on sporting goods

   B to become a professional baseball player

   C Doubleday to be remembered as a great man

   D Americans to know the truth

10 According to the article, when was the word "baseball" first mentioned?

 A 1639

 B 1700

 C 1774

 D 1839

11 What is this article **mostly** about?

 A whether baseball is the most popular sport

 B whether baseball was based on the game of rounders

 C whether baseball is really America's "National Pastime"

 D whether baseball was really invented in the United States

12 After reading the article, the reader could conclude that

 A baseball was actually invented in England

 B baseball was once more popular than it is today

 C Abner Doubleday probably did not invent baseball

 D the game of baseball has not been around very long

STOP

R.1.c

6 Understand Directions

Getting the Idea

When you try something new, like making a craft project or baking a delicious batch of cookies, you need to follow **directions** to successfully complete your task. Directions help you make sure that you have all the items you need before you start a task. They also guide you step-by-step through the whole project.

Directions can be called instructions or recipes. They are found in many places, including containers, cookbooks, and Web sites. Following directions exactly as they are written will help you successfully complete your task.

Read this sentence about making applesauce.

> Before adding the apples to the blender, you should first peel them. Then, have an adult remove their cores.

When reading directions, it is important to follow all of the steps in the correct order. This applesauce probably wouldn't taste as good if the hard apple core and seeds had been blended into it.

A great way to keep track of the steps is to pay close attention to words about the order of events. Look for words like *before, first, then, later, during,* and *after* to help you understand the directions.

Coached Example

Read this passage and answer the questions that follow.

Dough for Kids

Ingredients

1 cup flour
1/2 cup salt
1/2 cup very warm water
paint (if you would like)

Tools

large bowl
large wooden or plastic spoon
cookie cutters
rolling pin

Directions

1. Gently mix the flour and salt in the large bowl.
2. Add water to the mixture.
3. Mix with the spoon until the dough gets too hard to stir.
4. Continue mixing the ingredients with your hands until the dough sticks together.
5. Roll out dough with a rolling pin and cut shapes with cookie cutters.
6. Allow shapes to dry for two days.
7. Paint your dried creations, if you would like!

Thinking It Through

1. Where can you find a list of the different parts that make the dough?

   A. under the heading "Ingredients"

   B. under the heading "Tools"

   C. under step 3

   D. under step 5

   HINT *Tools* is a possibility, but it sounds like it only lists things that help you make the dough.

2. Which of these items is NOT needed to make the recipe work?

   A. flour

   B. large bowl

   C. water

   D. paint

   HINT Look for any notes the author may have included. What could you choose to make the dough without?

Coached Reading

DIRECTIONS
Read the passage below. While you are reading, look to the Reading Guide for tips.

Milk-Jug Birdhouse

Reading Guide

Materials:

Clean plastic milk jug, with screw-on lid
Thin rope or cord

Tools:

Sharp scissors (Adult help is needed for this tool.)
Permanent marker or grease pencil

Optional:

Nontoxic paints
Paintbrush

> What will you find under *Materials*? Is it like the *Ingredients* section in a recipe?

How to Make Your Birdhouse:

1. First, tie the rope to the handle of the jug. This will allow the house to be hung from a tree branch or a metal arm.
2. Use the marker or grease pencil to mark a spot for the birdhouse opening. This spot should be on the side of the jug opposite the handle. It should be about halfway down the jug.
3. With the help of an adult, cut a hole about one inch across at the spot you have marked.
4. Screw the lid on the top of the jug.
5. Paint your birdhouse with nontoxic paints, if you would like.
6. Finally, ask your adult helper to hang your birdhouse from a tree branch six to ten feet off the ground.

> What do the numbers tell you?

Independent Practice

DIRECTIONS
Use the passage to answer questions 1–4.

1. What tool is needed for this job?

   A. hammer

   B. rope

   C. scissors

   D. milk jug lid

2. Which item is not needed but may be used if desired?

   A. paint

   B. milk jug

   C. scissors

   D. rope

3. For which steps do you need an adult's help?

   A. steps 1 and 2

   B. steps 3 and 6

   C. steps 2 and 4

   D. steps 4 and 5

4. What does the picture show you?

   A. where to place the opening

   B. how to screw on the lid

   C. what designs to paint on the birdhouse

   D. how to use the scissors

7 Organizational Features

R.1.f, R.1.k

Getting the Idea

You read some books for fun, like novels or plays. But sometimes, you read to learn something—to get facts. Books like dictionaries, encyclopedias, and textbooks have facts. That's why you read them. These texts have **organizational features** that help you find what you are looking for.

The **title** is the name of the book. It tells you what the book is about or what you should use it for. So you can find it easily, the title appears on the book's cover. It usually appears on one of the inside pages, too.

Once you find the book you want, how do you find information inside it? You can use a table of a contents. A **table of contents** lists all the book's sections, or chapters, in order. Next to each chapter appears the page number where the chapter starts. Imagine you're looking at a guide for places to visit in New York City. The table of contents might look like this:

Like a table of contents, an **index** helps you find information. It lists pages where you can find subjects. It is usually found at the back of a text. To make it really easy to find subjects, an index lists subjects in alphabetical order. Look at the index for a book about bears.

Coached Example

DIRECTIONS
Read this index and answer the questions that follow.

black holes	53, 61
eclipses	19
galaxies	8, 43–47, 52
planets	20-25
solar systems	31–36, 58
stars	7, 11, 14–18

 Thinking It Through

1. On which page would you find information about eclipses?

   A. 7

   B. 19

   C. 36

   D. 58

   HINT Find the listing for *eclipses*. Then look at the page number beside it.

2. On page 8, you would find information about

   A. solar systems

   B. black holes

   C. planets

   D. galaxies

   HINT Look through the listings to find page 8. Then look to the left to see which subject appears on that page.

Lesson Practice

Coached Reading

DIRECTIONS

Read the table of contents below. While you are reading, look to the Reading Guide for tips.

Reading Guide

What do you think a *tuber* is? Look at the title of Chapter 1.

Annuals are flowers that bloom for just one year. *Perennials* flower year after year.

What do you think you would learn in this chapter?

Independent Practice

DIRECTIONS
Use the passage to answer questions 1–4.

1. Based on the table of contents, this book is MOSTLY about

    A. vegetables.

    B. flowers.

    C. gardening.

    D. bushes.

2. Which of these sentences would PROBABLY be found on page 40?

    A. "If you have a small area for a garden, do not plant flowers that will spread."

    B. "Everyone can learn how to successfully grow plants and vegetables."

    C. "Tubers grow well in cool climates."

    D. "Most people consider the tomato to be a vegetable."

3. You would PROBABLY use this book to find information about

    A. how to attract birds and butterflies.

    B. preparing soil for growing plants.

    C. recipes for vegetable dishes.

    D. how to make flower arrangements.

4. Based on the topics in the table of contents, what would be the BEST title for this book?

    A. Gardening for Beginners

    B. How to Prepare Vegetables

    C. Trimming Shrubs and Bushes

    D. Tools for Gardening

8 Text Features

R.1.k

Getting the Idea

When you flip through an informational book, you see that some words are bigger and bolder than others. They appear at the very beginning of sections. These words are **headings**, and they tell you when a new section is beginning. Headings tell you what each section of a book or long article is about. They help you quickly find information you need. Authors may also use **subheadings** to break the section under the heading into even smaller parts.

Like headings, **key words** may appear in bold type. This is often the case in textbooks. In articles, though, important words may not be bold. You will have to scan for words that will help you look for what you are trying to find. Think of a few main words about your topic and look for them in the text. Quickly read the first and last sentence of a paragraph. This can help you decide if you are in the right place, or if you should go on to another part of the article.

Graphics are diagrams or pictures that go along with words in a book. Graphics can be very useful. They help explain the text, or they show complex information in picture form. Graphics jump right out at you, so they are easy to find. They can tell you if the text in that section is likely to give the information you need.

Most graphics in books have **captions**. Captions are words beneath the picture that describe what the picture shows. For example, a caption underneath a map of our country might read "The United States of America."

Coached Example

DIRECTIONS
Read this passage from a book about animals and answer the questions that follow.

The Three Types of Horses

There are three types of horses. They share certain qualities. Each type also has qualities that make it unique.

Heavy Horses

The heavy horse gets its name from its great weight. Its body is long, and its back is wide. Because of their size and strength, heavy horses often pull plows and carriages.

Light Horses

Compared to heavy horses, light horses have short, narrow bodies. The shape of the back allows saddles to fit easily. Light horses are used for riding more than other kinds of horses.

Ponies

Ponies are the shortest type of horse. Because ponies are low to the ground, they are well-suited to child riders. Ponies are more sure-footed than the other types of horses. They also live longer than heavy horses or light horses.

Thinking It Through

1. What does the heading tell about the article?

   A. It will be about kinds of horses.

   B. It will be about famous horses.

   C. It will be about how to ride a horse.

   D. It will be about rodeo contests.

   HINT The main heading does not talk about famous animals, learning to ride, or rodeos.

2. Under which subheading would you find information about what large horses do?

   A. Heavy Horses

   B. Light Horses

   C. Ponies

   D. The Three Types of Horses

   HINT The first two subheadings describe sizes of horses. *Light Horses* and *Ponies* do not sound very big.

Coached Reading

DIRECTIONS
Read the passage below. While you are reading, look to the Reading Guide for tips.

The Virginia Opossum

1   The Virginia opossum is the only marsupial, or animal with a pouch, in North America. It has many other interesting qualities, too.

Physical Description

2   About the size of a large housecat, the opossum is grayish with a pointed face. Its tail can hold onto tree limbs. On its back feet, the opossum has a big toe that is like a thumb. This toe has no claw and can grasp branches.

Hind paw of opossum

Food

3   Opossums eat insects, mice, and lizards. They eat fruit and vegetables. Opossums also eat *carrion*, or dead animals.

Life Cycle

4   Usually, a Virginia opossum has seven to nine babies at a time. The tiny babies climb up the mother's fur into the pouch. There they grow for fifty-five to sixty days. Then they stay on the mother's back there for four to six weeks. After that, the babies go off on their own. Opossums usually live no more than eighteen months.

Behavior

5   When faced with a large predator, an opossum may pretend to be dead. It rolls over, becomes stiff, and its breathing becomes slow and shallow. Some animals will think it is dead and leave it alone.

Reading Guide

What does the title say this article will be about?

What does this graphic help you understand?

Where will you find information about how long Virginia opossums live?

Independent Practice

DIRECTIONS
Use the passage to answer questions 1–4.

1. In which section would you find information about what opossums eat?

   A. Physical Description

   B. Food

   C. Life Cycle

   D. Behavior

2. What is the purpose of the graphic?

   A. to make the page look nicer

   B. to show what the opossum's hind paw looks like

   C. to show how similar the opossum's paw is to a cat's paw

   D. to explain the opossum's life cycle

3. If you wanted to learn about how opossums protect themselves from other animals, which key word would you search for?

   A. predator

   B. branches

   C. marsupial

   D. housecat

4. Read this sentence.

   Opossums are nocturnal animals that usually prefer to live alone.

   This sentence would BEST fit under which heading?

   A. Physical Description

   B. Food

   C. Life Cycle

   D. Behavior

9 Graphic Organizers

R.1.l, R.2.p

Getting the Idea

Graphic organizers are charts or webs that help you arrange information. Let's look at some graphic organizers. Read this a paragraph about Sanjay.

> My alarm clock did not go off, so I kept snoozing until 7:15. I got up so late that I didn't have time for breakfast. I just threw on my clothes and brushed my teeth. I caught my 7:30 bus just in time. Boy, was I hungry by the time science class started at 8:45!

If you need to remember what happened to Sanjay, you can use a graphic organizer. A **chart**, or a table, shows information in columns and rows.

Time	Event
7:15	Sanjay woke up late.
7:30	Sanjay caught the bus.
8:45	Sanjay's science class began.

A **sequence chart** is used to show events in the order they happen.

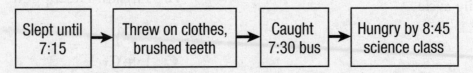

Another type of graphic organizer is called a web. A **web** has a main topic in the center, and ideas about the topic around it. Here is a web about the activities Sanjay does on a typical weekday.

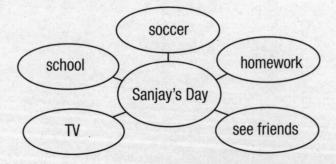

Coached Example

DIRECTIONS
Read this passage and answer the questions that follow.

Ada Johnson was born in Alberta, Canada, in 1904. She settled in the Boston area and married a local man, Henry Moriarty, in 1932. She worked as a telephone operator for a short time, and then she stopped working to raise five children. She died in 1993, when she was 89. Ada was my great-grandmother.

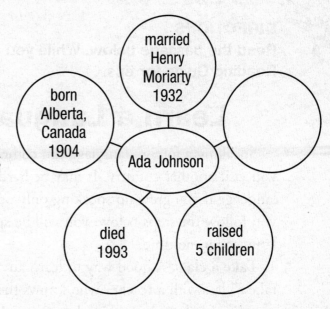

Thinking It Through

1. Which of the following belongs in the web?

    A. married at 28

    B. worked as a telephone operator

    C. had 4 girls and 1 boy

    D. was Canadian citizen

    HINT Think about what type of information is already in the web. It contains information about things Ada did. Ada's age at different stages is not mentioned, nor is her citizenship. Her children are already listed in the web, and their gender is not given in the article.

2. Look at this sequence chart.

    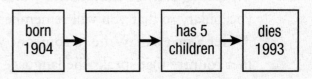

    Which of the following belongs in the empty box?

    A. ill 1992

    B. last child born 1951

    C. marries 1932

    D. does not finish high school

    HINT Think about the order of events. Only one choice fits in time order in the box.

Lesson Practice

Coached Reading

DIRECTIONS
Read the passage below. While you are reading, look to the Reading Guide for tips.

Learn a Language

Speaking a foreign language can come in handy when you visit another country. It may be hard to learn a language if you grew up speaking only one. However, if you follow the steps below, you will be speaking another language in no time.

1. **Take a class.** A good way to learn any language is to take a class with a teacher who knows the language. Pay attention and participate in class.

2. **Learn from speakers of the language.** Another great option is to learn from someone who speaks the language. Have conversations with that person. Meet with the person regularly to learn useful words. Pay attention to the vocabulary so that you will remember it.

3. **Get a pen pal.** Write to someone your age who lives in a country that speaks the language you are learning. When you write in another language, you practice your vocabulary and grammar. It also helps you remember vocabulary.

4. **Study vocabulary.** Start by learning useful words, like *house, mother, kitchen,* and *lunch.* Learn to ask questions, such as, "Where is the school?" Use this method:

  1. Say the word.   3. Use the word in a sentence.
  2. Write the word.   4. Repeat the word.

5. **Speak aloud and often.** Once you know a few words, practice speaking them aloud. This part can be scary, but just give it a try! It's very easy to forget what you've learned if you don't use it!

Reading Guide

What is this passage mostly about?

How could you put this information in a web?

Placing the steps in a sequence chart will help you understand and remember them.

Independent Practice

DIRECTIONS
Use the passage to answer questions 1–3.

1. Read the chart below.

Ways to Learn a Language
Take a class that teaches it.
Write to someone who speaks it.
?

Which sentence BEST completes the chart?

A. Listen to a song in it.

B. Speak out loud and often in it.

C. Find teachers who want to learn it.

D. Study famous people who speak it.

2. Here is a web about the passage.

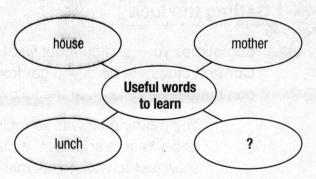

Which word could be added to this web?

A. basketball

B. saxophone

C. kitchen

D. flower

3. The chart below shows the order of steps to follow when studying vocabulary.

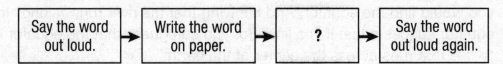

Which step BEST completes the chart?

A. Write a similar word.

B. Use the word in a sentence.

C. Say the meaning of the word.

D. Write the word on paper again.

10 Context Clues

Getting the Idea

Sometimes you can figure out what a word means using context clues. **Context clues** are hints you get from the words around the word you don't understand. Look at the following sentence.

> The morning air was so frigid he had to wear long underwear, a snowsuit, a parka, boots, mittens, and a scarf just to walk to his mailbox.

What if you don't know what the word *frigid* means? From context clues, you can tell that *frigid* is a word that describes the morning air. It must require a person to dress very warmly. It's a good guess that *frigid* means "extremely cold."

Some words are connected with a certain subject area, like geography or science. Look at the following sentence.

> From space, the river looks like a crack in the center of the earth. It runs along the equator.

The first sentence helps you picture the earth from space. When you read the word *equator* in the next sentence, you can look back at the first sentence. The phrase "in the center of the earth" suggests where you would find the equator. And knowing that the river runs "along" the equator suggests that it is a line. So, you can guess that the equator is "a line that runs across the center of the earth."

Coached Example

DIRECTIONS
Read this passage and answer the questions that follow.

One Thanksgiving, Uncle Mike visited us from Florida. He had never met our poodle, Fluffy, before. Uncle Mike spoiled her with treats and let her jump up on him. Fluffy hung around near Uncle Mike all day.

During dinner, Uncle Mike spilled gravy on his shirt. He started to rub it off with his napkin. Fluffy jumped up to lick the gravy from his napkin. She didn't stop there. She started to chew on the napkin. Uncle Mike tried to pull it from Fluffy's mouth, but Fluffy held fast.

Finally, my grandma took a piece of turkey smothered in gravy and waved it in front of Fluffy's face. The dog let go of the napkin and took the piece of turkey in her mouth instead. Fluffy was more interested in treats than in Uncle Mike.

Thinking It Through

1. What does *smothered* PROBABLY mean?

   A. covered

   B. messy

   C. fried

   D. smelly

   HINT Fluffy liked the gravy, so the grandma gave her something else to chew that had gravy on it. The word *smothered* has to do with what the grandma did to the piece of turkey.

2. Read this sentence from the passage.

   Uncle Mike tried to pull it from Fluffy's mouth, but Fluffy held fast.

   In this sentence, *fast* MOST LIKELY means

   A. loosely.

   B. tightly.

   C. quickly.

   D. gently.

   HINT The dog still held onto the napkin even when Uncle Mike tried to pull it away. Only one of the choices describes how the dog held onto the napkin.

Lesson Practice

Coached Reading

DIRECTIONS
Read the passage below. While you are reading, look to the Reading Guide for tips.

Henrietta de Beaulieu Dering Johnston: America's First Female Professional Artist

Reading Guide

1   Henrietta Johnston came to Charleston in 1707 with her husband. Mr. Johnston was a minister. He came to Charleston to work in the church, but he did not make much money. Henrietta was worried. "How will we support the family?" she asked herself.

> What is a *minister*? What clues explain this job?

2   She decided that she would work, too. "What can I do?" she wondered. Then she realized the answer. She could draw!

3   She earned her own income by becoming a society artist. Rich people paid her money to draw portraits of them. There were no cameras at the time. If a person wanted a picture, he or she had to hire someone to paint or draw it.

> Are there clues that tell what *income* means?

4   People who study art history say that Henrietta was the first artist to use pastels in America. Her art became very popular. A lot of people wanted her to draw pictures of them. This was good news for her because she had been dubious about her family's financial future. Her hard work and talent kept the family out of poverty. They had a rather nice life instead.

Independent Practice

DIRECTIONS
Use the passage to answer questions 1–4.

1. Based on context clues, what is a *minister*?

   A. someone who paints

   B. someone who draws pictures

   C. someone who works in a church

   D. someone who makes money

2. Read these sentences from the passage.

   Henrietta was worried. "How will we support the family?" she asked herself.

   Which meaning of *support* is used in these sentences?

   A. to hold something up

   B. to provide money for

   C. to comfort

   D. to put up with

3. Read this sentence from the passage.

   She earned her own income by becoming a society artist.

   What is *income*?

   A. money

   B. picture

   C. painting

   D. camera

4. Someone who is feeling *dubious* is

   A. angry.

   B. doubtful.

   C. relaxed.

   D. happy.

1 Review

Directions
Read this article. Then answer questions 1 through 5.

Take a Deep Breath

by Ben Molloy

You may not think about it much. It's not something you can see. But it's something you need. What is it? The air you breathe. How we breathe involves many organs—an entire system—in the body.

Becoming Aware of Breathing

Most of the time, you probably don't think about breathing. It's not something you do actively: it's involuntary. You breathe without thinking. What if you did think about breathing? How does air get through your body? Which parts of your body are involved in this process?

Starting the Process

To learn more about breathing, take a deep breath. What happens? First—and you can't feel this—a muscle just below your lungs moves down. What does this muscle do? It helps air enter your nose and mouth. That's the second part of breathing we're all aware of. Your mouth is responsible for warming the air you breathe and making it moist. That's why, especially when it's cold, the air you breathe out feels warm and damp. Your nose filters out any unwanted materials—things like tiny pieces of dust or dirt, so those materials can't get into your body.

Continuing Breathing

In the third step of breathing, the throat gets involved. The air moves down your throat and into your lungs. Then the lungs finalize the fourth and fifth steps of breathing. In the fourth step of breathing, the lungs take oxygen from the air and put it into the blood. In the fifth step they take carbon dioxide out of the blood.

Keeping It Going

That brings us to the final, or sixth, step of breathing: breathing out. When you exhale, air escapes your body. So does the carbon dioxide your lungs have taken from your blood. With this waste out of your system, you can keep right on breathing. So, take a deep breath—then let it out again!

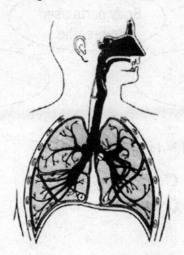

1 According to "Starting the Process," what is the first step of breathing?

   A Air enters the nose and mouth.

   B The nose filters out dust and dirt.

   C A muscle below the lungs moves down.

   D The mouth gives the air moisture and warmth.

2 Read these sentences from the article.

   Most of the time, you probably don't think about breathing. It's not something you do actively: it's involuntary.

The word "involuntary" in the second sentence **most likely** means

   A to do without thinking

   B to do something actively

   C to do something you do not want to do

   D to think about something before doing it

Go On

3 Here is a web about the article.

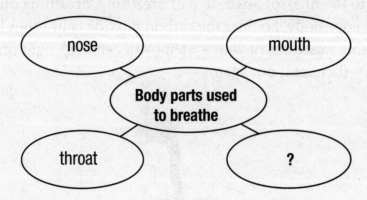

Which word could be added to this web?

A eyes **C** ears

B lungs **D** stomach

4 Look at the table of contents below.

On which page would you **most likely** find the article "Take a Deep Breath"?

A 1 **C** 34

B 14 **D** 50

5 What information can be found in the section "Keeping It Going"?

A the body parts used to take air in

B the fact that breathing is involuntary

C the last step of breathing or exhaling

D the way oxygen moves into the blood

Directions
Read this article. Then answer questions 6 through 10.

Marvelous Mosaics

by Tracy Pastorella

Mosaics are designs or images that are "built" out of tiny shapes. Usually, these tiny shapes are actually small tiles. The tiles can be squares, circles, or any other shape. They can be made of many different types of material. And mosaics may contain lots of different colors.

Mosaics have been made by people for a very long time. Some of the oldest mosaics were found on the floors of wealthy Greeks. They were made of natural pebbles. Black pebbles were mainly used for the background. White pebbles were used for figures. The mosaic designs usually included a simple picture or scene, like people hunting. These scenes were surrounded by several borders. This design gave these mosaics the look of a carpet.

Later, Greek mosaics had more detailed designs. They were made up of small cubes cut from stone. A few of the mosaics also contained pieces of colored glass. These new colors and materials allowed artists to be much more creative. There was almost no limit to the images that could be made.

Go On

Greek artists brought the art of mosaic-making to modern-day Italy. The Romans carried on the art. They made these beautiful designs on a much larger scale. Enormous buildings were given huge mosaic floors.

As time went on, mosaics were not just used for floors. They crept upward to the walls and ceilings of buildings. They became an important adornment in churches and palaces. Mosaics shining with gold covered the walls of buildings across Europe.

You don't need to be a professional artist to make a mosaic, though. You can create a great mosaic out of any small and flat object. Some good items to use are coins, colored paper, or buttons. For this mosaic, however, you will use brightly colored candy pieces.

Materials

- a multicolored assortment of small, flat candy pieces—you will need 1 or 2 large bags
- a piece of cardboard about the size of a magazine
- one jar of marshmallow crème
- a small bowl
- a small spoon

Procedure

1. Move the candy pieces around on the cardboard until you have created an image or design that you like. (Remember, the candy isn't stuck on the paper yet, so be careful not to move the pieces out of place.)

2. Use the spoon to put a little marshmallow crème in a small bowl.

3. Using the marshmallow crème as a kind of glue, use your fingers to slowly put at least a dime-sized amount of marshmallow crème under each piece and attach to the cardboard. (Be careful to use enough marshmallow crème so your pieces will stick.)

4. Repeat until all of the pieces have been stuck to the cardboard. Make sure you don't miss any pieces.

5. Wait overnight until all the crème has hardened, or the candy will fall out of place if you try to pick up the mosaic.

6. Enjoy your candy design!

6 What should you do **right after** moving the candy pieces onto cardboard in a design that you like?

A Spoon a little marshmallow crème into a bowl.
B Wait overnight until all the crème has hardened.
C Stick each candy piece with crème onto the cardboard.
D Place a small amount of marshmallow crème on each piece.

7 Look at the index below.

art
glass blowing 64, 72
mosaics 31–36
paintings 9, 54–58, 63
sculptures 42–47, 69

On which page would you find information about mosaics?

A 8
B 34
C 46
D 72

8 Read these sentences from the article.

They became an important adornment in churches and palaces. Mosaics shining with gold covered the walls of buildings across Europe.

Which word means about the same as "adornment"?

A signal
B painting
C structure
D decoration

Go On

9 What should you do **right before** sticking all the candy pieces onto cardboard?

    A Put a little marshmallow crème in a bowl.

    B Wait overnight until all the crème has hardened.

    C Stick a small amount of marshmallow crème onto each piece.

    D Move the pieces around until you have made a design you like.

10 Read the chart below.

Features of Early Greek Mosaics
They are made of natural pebble material.
They are colored black and white.
?

Which sentence **best** completes the chart?

    A They have very detailed designs.

    B They contain pieces of colored glass.

    C They show simple scenes with borders.

    D They are on the floor, walls, and ceilings.

STOP

CHAPTER 2

Literary Response and Expression

11 Make Inferences and Draw Conclusions

R.1.h, R.2.f

Getting the Idea

Sometimes ideas are implied. This means that writers don't state the ideas directly. They place clues or details throughout the text about the idea. You must study the clues to learn the idea. When you put the clues together, you make an inference or draw a conclusion.

An **inference** is an educated guess based on details in a passage, common sense, and personal knowledge. You can make inferences while you are reading. Read the passage below.

> The gray, rainy day matched Victoria's mood. She sat in her room with a box of tissues. The rain fell, and Victoria sniffled and wiped tears from her eyes.

This passage never says how Victoria feels. Rather, it includes hints about how she feels: the weather matches her mood, she has a box of tissues, and she is sniffling and crying. From these details, you can infer that Victoria probably feels sad.

A **conclusion** is a decision that a reader makes about the passage after reading it. It is based on details from the passage, as well as on any inferences made while reading. Read this example.

> John filled the tea kettle with water. Then, he placed the kettle on the stove. Next, John cracked two eggs into a frying pan. He placed the frying pan on the stove, too. John dropped two pieces of bread into the toaster.

The details in this passage describe John's actions: boiling water, frying eggs, and making toast. You can conclude that John is cooking breakfast.

Coached Example

DIRECTIONS
Read this passage and answer the questions that follow.

Fred loaded the tent and sleeping bags into the trunk of the car. The cooler was full of ice and food, and there were more boxes of snacks still in the house, ready to be brought out.

Fred ran through his checklist in his mind: bug spray, sunscreen, and first aid kit. He had packed all of these things in his backpack. But wait, he thought, what about his binoculars and bird guidebook? He ran upstairs to the den and got both.

The fishing poles were carefully strapped to the car's roof, and Fred's backpack was on the front seat. Now all that was left was to grab the compass and map his dad had given him, and he would be ready to leave.

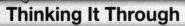

Thinking It Through

1. Which of the following will Fred PROBABLY do when he gets where he is going?

   A. go skiing

   B. watch a movie

   C. play baseball

   D. look for birds

   HINT Think about what Fred packs. He doesn't bring skis, a movie to watch, or a baseball mitt.

2. Where is Fred going?

   A. shopping

   B. to a baseball game

   C. camping

   D. to the movies

   HINT Think about all the clues together. Fred would not need food, clothes, bug spray, a tent, and the other things to go shopping, to a baseball game, or to the movies.

Lesson Practice

Coached Reading

DIRECTIONS
Read the passage below. While you are reading, look to the Reading Guide for tips.

Ray's Ride

Reading Guide

1   Ray drove down the quiet stretch of road all by himself. It had gotten dark and cold very quickly. He was surprised because it had been so sunny and bright just an hour or so ago. The wind blew in his hair as he sped along.

2   Suddenly, he felt a jerk, then a shudder, and then a sputter. He glanced down and squinted at the dimly lit display. He realized that the needle had moved to the *E* on the dial. "Uh-oh," he thought to himself. "I probably should've stopped at that service station in the last town."

> Do you think Ray should worry about the sounds his vehicle is making? Why or why not?

> Why should Ray have stopped at the service station in the last town?

3   Ray pulled over and stepped off his vehicle. He put the kickstand down so it wouldn't topple over. The headlight gave off enough light to let him see that there was nothing around but sand. There weren't even any plants! Then he heard a howling sound off in the distance. He knew he was in trouble.

> Why did Ray get off of his vehicle?

Independent Practice

DIRECTIONS
Use the passage to answer questions 1–4.

1. What happened to Ray's vehicle?

   A. It had a flat tire.

   B. It ran out of gas.

   C. It caught fire.

   D. Part of its engine broke.

2. The howling sound in this story is MOST LIKELY coming from

   A. a person.

   B. a radio.

   C. wild coyotes.

   D. elephants.

3. Why did Ray know he was in trouble?

   A. He did not see plants.

   B. He saw a lot of sand.

   C. He knew he was going to be late.

   D. He knew there was no help nearby.

4. What does the *E* on the dial mean?

   A. electric

   B. empty

   C. excellent

   D. entrance

12 Make Predictions

R.2.f

Getting the Idea

Have you ever tried to guess what was going to happen in the future? When you make a **prediction**, you make a guess about what will most likely happen next.

You can make predictions about what a character will do next, what will happen to a character next, how a character will react, or what event will happen next.

The most important thing to remember when making predictions is that a prediction is not just a guess. It is a guess that you make for a reason. It is what is likely to happen, not something that you wish would happen.

There are different situations in which you would make a prediction. Let's take a look at a few of them.

Possible Times When A Prediction Could Be Made

What You Observe	What You Can Predict
A character has acted the same way throughout the story.	A character that has been mean will probably continue to do mean things.
The narrator has described an event of which the character is not aware.	The event will probably affect what the character thinks and does.
You have previous knowledge about what is happening to a character.	If the character is doing something you have done, you can guess what he or she will do next.

Coached Example

DIRECTIONS
Read this passage and answer the questions that follow.

Maddy chewed her lip, watching to see who would get the ball. It was Vicki! Vicki was Maddy's best friend. Things had been tough at home lately for Vicki, and basketball was how she kept her mind off her problems. Maddy had come to every game this season to show support.

Vicki raced down the court, dribbling rapidly. Everything was going perfectly. The score was tied. Just one more basket to win!

Maddy crossed her fingers. She could hardly stand the excitement. She perched on the edge of her seat, barely touching the bleachers. She was so nervous that she jiggled her legs and drummed her hands on her thighs. The tension was building!

Vicki focused on moving down the court. She kept her eye on her goal as she ran. She approached the hoop and aimed the ball. Everything felt like it was happening in slow motion.

Thinking It Through

1. What will Vicki PROBABLY do next?

   A. She will run out the door.

   B. She will throw the ball.

   C. She will ask her coach what to do.

   D. She will call a time-out.

   HINT Vicki has already approached the hoop and aimed the ball. Only one of these choices is a reasonable thing for Vicki to do.

2. What will Maddy PROBABLY do next?

   A. She will leave before the end of the game.

   B. She will phone Vicki's parents to tell them about the game.

   C. She will show her excitement when Vicki throws the ball.

   D. She will boo the other team if Vicki's side does not win.

   HINT Maddy probably will not leave early, because she wants to show her support. She could call Vicki's parents or boo the other side, but there are no clues that suggest she would do this.

Lesson Practice

Coached Reading

DIRECTIONS
Read the passage below. While you are reading, look to the Reading Guide for tips.

Eddie's Trip

Reading Guide

1   Stan and Breanne were having lunch. When dessert arrived, Stan said, "Did I tell you about what Eddie is up to?"

2   Breanne shook her head. "He's heading out on a winter fishing trip to the mountains with his brother," Stan explained.

3   "Wow, Eddie is quite the fisherman, isn't he?" Breanne said.

4   "Yeah," Stan laughed, spooning up ice cream. "He could catch a fish in a mud puddle. But I wouldn't want to go hiking through the snow to a frozen lake out there," he added, "in the middle of nowhere."

> Eddie does a lot of fishing. What does this tell about what is likely to happen on his trip?

5   "Hey, many people enjoy ice fishing," Breanne said, swallowing the last bit of pie. "They camp in shelters right on the frozen lake. They carve a hole through to the water inside the shelters, and fish indoors."

6   Stan nodded with a smile. But he thought to himself, *Well, I'd still never do it!*

7   Breanne put her napkin on the table. "We should do this again," she said. "Next time, lunch is on you."

8   Stan nodded and smiled. He looked forward to his next talk and his next lunch with Breanne.

> Will they have lunch again soon? Are there clues that suggest an answer?

Independent Practice

DIRECTIONS
Use the passage to answer questions 1–5.

1. What will the server PROBABLY do next?

    A. He will yell at them for talking too loudly.

    B. He will scold them for eating too quickly.

    C. He will bring the bill.

    D. He will bring more food.

2. What will Breanne PROBABLY do next?

    A. pay the bill

    B. run out without paying

    C. ask for more pie

    D. ask Stan to pay

3. When Eddie gets to the lake, what do you predict he will do first?

    A. set up a shelter

    B. drop his fishing line into the water

    C. turn around and go home

    D. walk to the store

4. What will Eddie PROBABLY do during his trip?

    A. build a log cabin

    B. join Stan and Breanne for lunch

    C. go snowboarding

    D. catch a lot of fish

5. Do you think Stan and Breanne will have lunch again soon or not? List two reasons for your prediction.

_____

_____

_____

_____

_____

13 Character

R.2.i, R.2.j

Getting the Idea

Characters are the people, animals, or objects a story is about. When you read, you should pay close attention to the way a character acts. The way he or she acts will tell you how the character feels. Once you understand how a character feels, you will understand the reasons for that character's actions. This will help you understand the story better.

Usually, an author doesn't simply tell you a character is angry, sad, or happy. You have to look at the way a character behaves to figure it out. Much like real people, characters in stories act and speak in certain ways. These patterns are called **traits**. Traits help us understand characters and group them as types. For example, characters who help people are heroes. Characters who hurt people are villains. Different types of characters make stories more interesting.

Keep in mind that characters may not have the same traits throughout a story. Events in the story may cause characters to change or develop. In a book-length story, a character might change as he or she grows up.

Read the following passage, and think about character traits.

> *Crack!* went the bat as it connected with the speeding ball. Kevin beamed. Another home run! As he turned and headed back to the bench, Luis caught his eye. Luis was sulking on the bench. "Hey, Luis!" he called to the other boy. "I'm tired of batting. Why don't you take a turn?" Instantly, Luis smiled. It would be a good workout after all.

Think about why Kevin does what he does. Would a mean or a selfish character offer Luis batting practice? Not likely. Kevin is kind; he is willing to help his friend.

Coached Example

Read this passage and answer the questions that follow.

Louise looked around the locker room. Her teammates sat with their heads down. They were breathing hard and sweating. Even Coach Laverty had a disappointed look on her face. Louise could not stand it anymore. She stood and cleared her throat.

"The game is not over," Louise said. "We are only losing by six points. This is the championship game. We have come too far this season to give up."

Louise clapped her hands. Slowly, her teammates lifted their heads. They began to clap, too. Coach Laverty smiled at Louise. When halftime was over, the players left the locker room. They were confident and excited again.

Thinking It Through

1. Louise is a character who

   A. gives up easily.

   B. is very hopeful.

   C. likes to joke.

   D. studies too much.

   HINT Consider Louise's words and actions in the passage.

2. Louise's speech is appropriate because

   A. she is much older than all of the other girls on her team.

   B. her team is losing at halftime of the championship game.

   C. the referee did a poor job during the first half of the game.

   D. Coach Laverty never speaks to the girls at halftime.

   HINT When and where does this story take place?

Lesson Practice

Coached Reading

DIRECTIONS
Read the passage below. While you are reading, look to the Reading Guide for tips.

The Mule Egg

Reading Guide

1   When Jimmy was sick, his aunt sent him a fruit basket. The basket had many treats. It also had something Jimmy had never seen before. It looked like a small, hairy bowling ball.

> What does this gift show about Jimmy's aunt?

2   He asked his brother, Matt, "Do you have any idea what this thing is?"

3   Matt knew it was a coconut, but he wanted to have some fun. "That's a mule egg," he said. "Take it into your room and sit on it. If you do that for a few weeks, a mule will hatch from it!" Jimmy had never seen a real mule, but he always wanted a pet. So he carried the coconut into his room and sat on it. He did this every day for a few weeks, with no result. Finally, he went back to Matt and told him nothing was happening.

> What trait does Matt show here?

4   "I guess you got a dud," he said.

5   Upset, Jimmy went outside and kicked the coconut into the bushes. Just then, a rabbit scooted out. Seeing the bunny hop away, and thinking it must be a mule, Jimmy chased after it, shouting, "Hey, get back here! Don't you know that I'm your father?"

Independent Practice

DIRECTIONS
Use the passage to answer questions 1–4.

1. Which word BEST describes Jimmy's aunt?

   A. kind

   B. nervous

   C. angry

   D. sick

2. How is Jimmy different from Matt?

   A. He is smarter than Matt.

   B. He is bigger than Matt.

   C. He is healthier than Matt.

   D. He is more easily fooled than Matt.

3. What kind of person is Matt?

   A. someone who studies hard

   B. some who is thoughtful

   C. someone who likes playing pranks

   D. someone who always tells the truth

4. How does Jimmy MOST LIKELY feel when he sees the rabbit hopping in the bushes?

   A. He is excited that the egg had hatched.

   B. He is amused at his brother's trick.

   C. He is angry that his brother tricked him.

   D. He is confused because he thought mules were bigger.

14 Sequence and Plot

R.2.i, R.2.j

Getting the Idea

Stories, like a lot of things, follow an order. They must have a beginning, a middle, and an end. This order is called **sequence**. For stories to make sense, the sequence must make sense. Take a story in which a boy bakes a cake with his father. The two can't put the cake in the oven until they've made the batter, for instance.

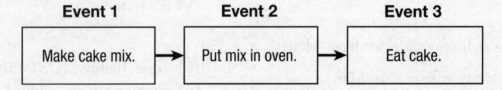

Event 1	Event 2	Event 3
Make cake mix.	Put mix in oven.	Eat cake.

In simple stories, the three parts of the **plot** usually happen in order. You find out what the **conflict**, or main problem, of the story is soon after you start reading. In the middle part of your reading, you see how characters try to solve the problem. At the end, you find out whether they were successful, and what happened. This is the **resolution** of the conflict.

The chart below shows how this works. As you'll see, something important happens in each of the three main parts of the plot.

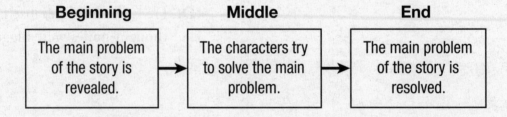

Beginning	Middle	End
The main problem of the story is revealed.	The characters try to solve the main problem.	The main problem of the story is resolved.

Coached Example

DIRECTIONS
Read this passage and answer the questions that follow.

Kanati's Son

adapted from a Native American folktale

Long ago, a hunter named Kanati lived on a mountain. His son played each day by the river. One day, the elders of the tribe heard two boys playing by the river, but they could only see Kanati's son. Concerned, that night they told Kanati what they had heard and seen. Kanati was puzzled. He knew his son played alone. There were no other boys in the tribe.

That night, Kanati approached his son. "But I do have a friend," the boy told his father. "He comes from the water."

The next day, Kanati watched as his son played by the water. Sure enough, before long, another boy appeared from the water! It was Adawehi—magic boy! And so the mystery was solved.

Thinking It Through

1. Read the sequence chart below.

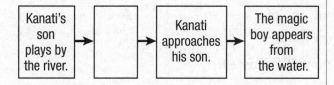

Kanati's son plays by the river. → [ ] → Kanati approaches his son. → The magic boy appears from the water.

Which event should go in the second box?

A. The elders speak with Kanati.

B. Kanati's son speaks with the elders.

C. The elders meet the magic boy.

D. Kanati plays in the water.

HINT What happens to make Kanati approach his son? Who delivers news to Kanati?

2. In which part of the story does the resolution take place?

A. The magic boy appears from the water.

B. Kanati's son plays by the river.

C. Kanati approaches his son.

D. The elders speak with Kanati.

HINT The elders do speak with Kanati, Kanati approaches his son, and Kanati's son plays again by the river. But these do not solve the problem in the story.

Lesson Practice

Coached Reading

DIRECTIONS
Read the passage below. While you are reading, look to the Reading Guide for tips.

The Night Before

1   Marla had been studying for hours, and her eyelids felt heavy. The science test that she was taking the next day was very important, so she wanted to go over everything one more time. Unfortunately, her brain was no longer cooperating. She knew she needed a break.

2   Downstairs, Teddy sat playing video games. Teddy had to take the same science test. Though he was Marla's twin brother, Teddy did not share her love of studying. In fact, Teddy hated to study, and his grades showed it. Marla came in and asked what he was doing.

3   "I'm studying," Teddy joked.

4   "I can't believe you," Marla said. "You know the test tomorrow is really important, right?"

5   "Important to you," Teddy said. "I'm not too concerned. I bet I do better than you on the test."

6   "It's a bet," Marla answered. "The winner has to do the other's chores for a week."

7   Marla and Teddy shook hands. With that, Marla grabbed a pack of crackers from the kitchen and returned upstairs.

8   The next day, she went into the test feeling confident. When she got an A, she knew she had earned it, just as Teddy had earned his F and a ticket to summer school. She also knew that she did not have any chores to do for a week.

Reading Guide

What is the problem that Marla faces?

How is Teddy's behavior different from Marla's?

Why does Marla pass and Teddy fail?

Independent Practice

DIRECTIONS
Use the passage to answer questions 1–4.

1. The first event in this passage's plot is

   A. Marla takes her science test.

   B. Teddy fakes being sick.

   C. Teddy plays video games.

   D. Marla takes a study break.

2. What is the main conflict in this passage?

   A. Marla wants to do well on the test.

   B. Teddy does not like to study.

   C. Teddy and Marla are twins.

   D. Marla is very hungry and sleepy.

3. Which event takes place RIGHT AFTER Marla and Teddy shake on the bet?

   A. Marla falls asleep.

   B. Marla gets a snack.

   C. Teddy decides to study.

   D. The twins take the test.

4. The resolution of this story is that

   A. Teddy goofs off instead of studying.

   B. Marla and Teddy make a bet.

   C. Marla passes the test and wins the bet.

   D. Teddy buys a new video game.

15 Setting

R.2.j

Getting the Idea

Almost every story you read will have characters. Stories have another important element: setting. **Setting** is the time and place in which the story happens. Basically, the setting is a story's "when" and "where." The time and place when a story happens can affect the kind of story it is. A story set on a pirate ship on the ocean during the 1800s, for instance, would probably be an adventure story. A story set in a haunted house would probably be a ghost story.

Sometimes, an author tells you what the setting is. Other times, the author gives you clues to help you figure out the setting. Here are some examples of things to look for.

Clues to the Setting
the clothes that characters are wearing
the things that characters are doing (or not doing)
the types of machines that are (or are not) mentioned or used
mentions of historical events (such as a war or the discovery of America) or historical figures (such as George Washington or King Henry VIII)

Read the following paragraph, and try to figure out the setting.

> A cool wind rustled through the trees overhead. Rosa could hear the tree frogs chirping. The wind shifted and ruffled the canvas of her tent. Through the space between the tent's flaps, Rosa could see the stars twinkling. The clouds moved across the sky. They gave glimpses of the nearly full, bright moon.

This paragraph gives you a few clues about setting. First, think about the "when" clues. You know the stars and moon are out, so it must be nighttime. What about the "where" clues? The trees, frogs, and tent are all "where" clues. Rosa must be camping outside.

Coached Example

DIRECTIONS
Read this passage and answer the questions that follow.

"I mean, come on, Mom," Marcus protested in front of the building. "You got me up early just to come here?" He sighed and trudged up the steps. "You know I'd rather sleep late on Saturday."

His mother smiled and ruffled his hair. "It's not so bad," she said. "You got to have breakfast from the drive-through doughnut stand!"

"But you know I'm not into places like this. They're old. And all they have is old things."

"Now, Marcus," his mother replied patiently. "This is the best place to learn about New York history. Besides," she continued, "your report is due in two days. What better place to get all the information you need?"

Thinking It Through

1. When does this passage PROBABLY take place?

   A. in the morning

   B. at lunchtime

   C. after school

   D. after dinner

   HINT Look for time clues. Marcus has recently eaten breakfast, so it's not lunchtime or after dinner. He mentions Saturday, so there is no school.

2. Which of the following BEST describes where this passage takes place?

   A. in a school library

   B. at a historical museum

   C. in a gymnasium

   D. at a lumber store

   HINT Marcus and his mother are not at school, because it is Saturday. A gymnasium would not have old things. A lumber store is probably not a place where Marcus could get information for a school report.

Lesson Practice

Coached Reading

DIRECTIONS
Read the passages below. While you are reading, look to the Reading Guide for tips.

Stefan's Big Question

Reading Guide

1   Stefan sat at his desk and read the question over and over. He just couldn't figure it out! Finally, the bell rang, and he had to turn in his test paper. After everyone else left, he went up to the teacher and asked her about the question.

2   "I'm usually a whiz at math," he said. "But I just can't figure out this one question."

3   The teacher looked at the problem, and then her face turned red. "I know why you couldn't figure it out," she told him. "I made a mistake when I wrote it!" The next day, the teacher announced that the one question would not count. Stefan was very happy to see that he got a 98.

> What clues tell you where and when this story happens?

Stranded

1   Malik trudged through the icy wilderness. The frigid wind blasted him, stinging his face. "This blizzard is just too strong," he thought to himself. "They won't be sending out any rescue helicopters tonight. I'd better find a warm, safe place to spend the night."

2   He found a large mound of snow and began digging a hole in the side. It took a long time, but he was able to make a space big enough to crawl into. "This will have to do until morning," he told himself.

> What are the *where* and *when* clues in this passage?

Independent Practice

DIRECTIONS
Use the passages to answer questions 1–4.

1. Where does the first passage MOST LIKELY take place?

    A. in a library

    B. at a circus

    C. on a mountain

    D. in a classroom

2. When does the second passage MOST LIKELY take place?

    A. in the recent past

    B. during the Revolutionary War

    C. during the time of dinosaurs

    D. in pioneer times

3. Which word in the second passage reveals the setting?

    A. wilderness

    B. helicopters

    C. mound

    D. warm

4. How is the setting in the first passage different from the setting in the second passage?

    A. The first passage takes place in the summer, and the second passage takes place in the winter.

    B. The first passage takes place in a school, and the second passage takes place at home.

    C. The first passage takes place indoors, and the second passage takes place outdoors.

    D. The first passage takes place in the 1800s, and the second passage takes place in the 1920s.

16 Theme

R.2.i, R.2.j, R.3.a

Getting the Idea

You have already learned that the main idea is what the passage is all about. This lesson covers **theme**, or the main message an author tries to give the reader in a passage.

Think about how the two are different. A passage may be about working, for example. That's the main idea. But if the author writes about how you should always do a good job, that's the theme.

Here are some common themes:

- Honesty is the best policy.
- Giving is more important than receiving.
- Don't be afraid to try something new.

Read the following paragraph, and try to figure out the theme.

> "Of course I'm an excellent swimmer," the monkey said to the dolphin as he perched on the edge of the boat. "Watch this!" he cried and jumped into the water. It wasn't long, though, before the monkey was thrashing about. Soon, the dolphin was nosing him back into the boat. "I didn't think monkeys could swim," the dolphin said.

Think about the lesson the monkey learned. Did he try to be something he was not? What happened? That tells you the theme of this passage: don't pretend to be something you're not.

Sometimes a story can have more than one theme. The key to figuring out the theme is to make sure it is supported by what happens in the story. Often, the theme will not be directly stated in a story. The reader has to decide what the theme is after thinking carefully about the story's characters and events.

Coached Example

DIRECTIONS
Read this passage and answer the questions that follow.

In the spring, a farmer went to visit one of his daughters. She had just married a gardener. "How are the vegetables?" the farmer asked upon arriving. "They're doing well," the daughter replied. "We just need one good shower so they can continue to grow."

"Well, here's a watering can," the farmer said. "Maybe this will help." He hummed as he left. He wanted his daughter to be happy.

Later, the farmer visited his other daughter. She was a potter and made lovely bowls and pitchers. "And how are things with you?" he asked.

"Just fine," she said. "But they would be even better if the sun would continue to shine and dry my pottery."

"Well, there's not much I can do about that," the farmer sighed. "One out of two will have to be enough for now."

"Don't worry," the daughter replied with a smile. "Things could always be worse."

Thinking It Through

1. Which of the following BEST describes the theme of this passage?

   A. You can only do one thing at a time.

   B. Only do the things you like.

   C. You can't always make everyone happy.

   D. Be careful what you wish for.

   HINT Think about what the farmer wants and what he realizes. The story is not about trying to do more than one thing or doing what you like. It does not have a warning.

2. Which other theme could fit this passage?

   A. Appreciate the things you have.

   B. Making pottery is a waste of time.

   C. Some people never have luck.

   D. Farming is hard work.

   HINT Think about what the last part of this passage is trying to teach you. It does not make a judgment about making pottery or farming. It doesn't talk about luck.

Lesson Practice

Coached Reading

DIRECTIONS
Read the passage below. While you are reading, look to the Reading Guide for tips.

Where are the Snags?

Reading Guide

1   Before there were airplanes and automobiles, many goods were shipped by boat. The problem with shipping things by boat was that many rivers have clusters of rocks and branches. The boatmen called these places "snags." If a boat hit a snag, it could get stuck. If it hit a really bad snag, it could even sink!

2   One day Boss Twill was interviewing people to pilot one of his boats. All day long, he talked to people who were not experienced. Finally, at the end of the day, a strange-looking man in a wrinkled suit came in.

3   Boss Twill asked, "Are you familiar with this river? Do you know where the snags are?"

4   "Well," the man said. "I'm familiar with the river, but I don't really know where the snags are."

5   Boss Twill rolled his eyes, and said, "Why should I hire you if you don't know where the snags are?"

6   The man got a serious look, then leaned forward and replied, "Because I know where the snags aren't, and that's where I sail!"

7   He got the job.

As you read, ask yourself: What lesson does Boss learn?

Is this a clue to the theme?

Independent Practice

DIRECTIONS
Use the passage to answer questions 1–4.

1. Which of the following is a theme of this story?

   A. You should not be too quick to judge people.

   B. Boats are not a good way to transport goods.

   C. Anybody can pilot a boat.

   D. Boss Twill owns a boat company.

2. What is one lesson of this story?

   A. You should always wear your best clothes to a job interview.

   B. People who own boat companies are not honest.

   C. If you can't see something, then it's not a problem.

   D. A different way of looking at things can work just as well.

3. What is one more lesson of this story?

   A. Real boatmen act strangely.

   B. It takes experience to pilot a boat.

   C. People who pilot boats have easy jobs.

   D. Boats are better than airplanes and automobiles.

4. What does Boss Twill learn in this story?

   A. how to pilot a boat

   B. how many snags there are

   C. how dangerous rivers are

   D. to think twice before he judges someone

2 Review

Directions
Read this story. Then answer questions 1 through 6.

The Little Pink Rosebud

retold by Sara Cone Bryant

Once there was a little pink Rosebud, and she lived down in a little dark house under the ground. One day she was sitting there, all by herself, and it was very still. Suddenly, she heard a little TAP, TAP, TAP, at the door.

"Who is that?" she said.

"It's the Rain, and I want to come in," said a soft, sad, little voice.

"No, you can't come in," the little Rosebud said.

By and by she heard another little TAP, TAP, TAP on the window pane.

"Who is there?" she said.

The same soft little voice answered, "It's the Rain, and I want to come in!"

"No, you can't come in," said the little Rosebud.

Then it was very still for a long time. At last, there came a little rustling, whispering sound, all round the window: RUSTLE, WHISPER, WHISPER.

"Who is there?" said the little Rosebud.

"It's the Sunshine," said a little, soft, cheery voice, "and I want to come in!"

"N—no," said the little pink rose, "you can't come in." And she sat still again.

Pretty soon she heard the sweet little rustling noise at the key-hole.

"Who is there?" she said.

"It's the Sunshine," said the cheery little voice, "and I want to come in, I want to come in!"

"No, no," said the little pink rose, "you cannot come in."

By and by, as she sat so still, she heard TAP, TAP, TAP, and RUSTLE, WHISPER, RUSTLE, all up and down the window pane, and on the door, and at the key-hole.

"WHO IS THERE?" she said.

"It's the Rain and the Sun, the Rain and the Sun," said two little voices, together, "and we want to come in! We want to come in! We want to come in!"

"Dear, dear!" said the little Rosebud, "if there are two of you, I s'pose I shall have to let you in."

So she opened the door a little wee crack, and in they came. And one took one of her little hands, and the other took her other little hand, and they ran, ran, ran with her, right up to the top of the ground. Then they said,—

"Poke your head through!"

So she poked her head through; and she was in the midst of a beautiful garden. It was springtime, and all the other flowers had their heads poked through; and she was the prettiest little pink rose in the whole garden!

1 Which word **best** describes the little Rosebud?

A mean
B lonely
C bashful
D friendly

2 This story **mostly** takes place

A in a flower shop
B in a big city
C in the sky
D in a garden

Go On

3 Why do the Rain and Sun want to get to the little Rosebud?

    A They want to frighten her.

    B They want to be her friends.

    C They want to clean her house.

    D They want to help her grow.

4 What will **most likely** happen next in the story?

    A The little Rosebud will return to her house.

    B The little Rosebud will speak with the Wind.

    C The little Rosebud will get bigger and bloom.

    D The little Rosebud will shout at the Rain and Sun.

5 Which event happens **first** in the story?

    A The Sun knocks on the little Rosebud's door.

    B The Rain knocks on the little Rosebud's door.

    C The little Rosebud tells the Sun it cannot come in.

    D The little Rosebud tells the Rain it cannot come in.

6 What is this story **mostly** about?

    A a rosebud who is afraid of new things

    B a rosebud who is mean and selfish

    C a rosebud who does not like gardens

    D a rosebud who does not have any friends

Directions
Read this story. Then answer questions 7 through 12.

Shadow Dancing

by Maya Medina

Edie was always excited when she first walked into the studio for dance class. She was only in the beginner class, but she loved to dance and practiced every day.

A month before the annual recital, Miss Eileen asked Edie to stay and watch the advanced class. Edie paid close attention to how her friend Alice, a fifth-grader, and the other girls danced.

Edie couldn't believe how talented the older girls were. Rebecca Stevens, a sixth-grader, would be dancing a solo. She could balance on one toe. She had even been allowed to audition for the main role in the City Ballet's *Nutcracker* this year.

Miss Eileen had chosen Alice to be the understudy for Rebecca. During rehearsals, Alice danced behind Rebecca almost like her shadow. Every move Rebecca made, Alice made right behind her. By following her, Alice could learn the part. If something came up to keep Rebecca out of the show, Alice would be ready to step in.

After the class was over, Miss Eileen walked over to Edie. She smiled and said "Edie, you have learned enough to join the class. This means you can be in the recital, too. But you'll have to work hard to learn the steps."

Edie looked around at all the older dancers. They were so strong and so experienced. She asked, "Do you think the others will mind that I'm not as good as them?"

Miss Eileen smiled. "Every dancer here was once the newest and least experienced in the group."

Go On

As Edie and Alice were walking home, Edie asked lots of questions about the performance. Then it hit her. She would be dancing in front of other people for the first time. What if she made a mistake?

Edie asked Alice, "Does anyone ever get too nervous at the last minute?"

Alice smiled. "I think everyone does. It's called 'stage fright.' I used to be afraid to perform. Then Miss Eileen taught me a great trick to keep me from worrying. She taught me to stand behind an older student. If I forgot any of the moves, I could just copy her. I'm sure you can stand behind me on stage. That way, if you forget something, you'll have me to follow." Edie was relieved.

When Edie showed up for the advanced class the next day, all of the dancers were buzzing. Rebecca had won the role in *The Nutcracker* with the City Ballet! That meant Alice would have to take her place in the upcoming show.

Alice didn't seem very happy about the news, though. She quietly danced her way through class. Alice didn't say a word on the walk home. Suddenly, she whispered to Edie. "Rebecca is so talented. She's the best 11-year-old dancer in the state. It would take me years to catch up with her."

Edie remembered what Miss Eileen had told her. Turning to Alice, she said, "Remember, every dancer was a beginner at some point… even Rebecca."

Alice was still feeling nervous. "I'm afraid that I won't be able to remember the really fast steps. What if I make a mistake?"

Edie had an idea. "Alice, what if you imagine that you are standing behind Rebecca when you do your solo?"

Looking at Edie, Alice smiled a little. "I'm not sure, but I'll think about it."

The night of the show, Edie danced in the back row. She followed the whole routine perfectly. When the group dance was over, it was time for Alice's solo. The music began. She began to move slowly. Then she spun like a feather through the air. She leapt across the stage and landed gently on one foot. The audience roared.

After the show, Miss Eileen told everyone how proud she was. Looking over at Alice, she said, "You were great."

Alice looked over at Edie and smiled. "It was almost like Rebecca was up there on stage with me," Alice said. Edie knew exactly what she meant.

7 Rebecca needs an understudy because

  A other dancers can learn from her
  B she cannot dance the part by herself
  C she might dance in *The Nutcracker*
  D the part requires two dancers to dance at once

8 Which sentence from the story **best** describes Alice's attitude when she found out she would be dancing the solo?

  A "Looking at Edie, Alice smiled a little."
  B "Alice didn't seem very happy about the news, though."
  C "She would be dancing in front of other people for the first time."
  D "That meant Alice would have to take her place in the upcoming show."

9 The sequence chart below shows the order of events in the story.

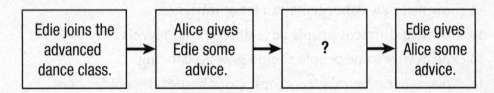

Which event **best** completes the chart?

  A Alice dances the solo perfectly.
  B Miss Eileen gives Edie some advice.
  C Rebecca auditions for a starring role.
  D Alice takes over Rebecca's solo.

Go On

10 The main characters have **most likely** learned that

    A meeting challenges can be rewarding

    B making mistakes can be embarrassing

    C practice does not always make perfect

    D inexperienced beginners make the best dancers

11 Why does Edie dance in the back row the night of the show?

    A She can hide her mistakes that way.

    B She is not allowed to stand anywhere else.

    C She can copy the other dancers most easily from there.

    D She does not have to worry about anyone seeing her there.

12 Why does the author **most likely** include information about older dancers and newer ones?

    A to show that new dancers make a lot of mistakes

    B to show that different people have different skill levels

    C to explain why some people should give up dancing

    D to explain that newer dancers must work harder than older ones

STOP

CHAPTER

3 Critical Analysis and Evaluation

17 Author's Purpose

R.3.a

Getting the Idea

People read for different reasons. Sometimes, you want to read something for fun. Other times, you read to find information for a school report. Maybe you read to find out how to do something.

Just as readers read for different reasons, writers write for different reasons. Some authors want to tell you a story that makes you laugh. Some want to give you information about a topic. Some want to tell you how to fix a car.

The reason an author writes is called the **author's purpose**. The most common purposes are to inform, persuade, and entertain.

Author's Purpose	Types of Texts
to inform	newspapers, magazines, encyclopedias, textbooks, how-to guides
to persuade	essays, editorials, advertisements
to entertain	novels, stories, poems, plays

Readers need to be able to recognize an author's purpose. This helps you better understand and judge what the writing says. To figure out the author's purpose, ask yourself what the writer wants you to think, feel, or do when you read. Usually, the way you feel is related to the author's purpose.

Coached Example

DIRECTIONS
Read this passage and answer the questions that follow.

High-speed trains have different names in different countries. In France they are called TGV, which stands for *trains à grande vitesse*. In England they are called HSR, which stands for "high-speed rail." And in Japan they are called *shinkansen*, or "bullet trains."

The bullet train was introduced in 1964. It was the world's first high-speed electric train, and it went as fast as 125 miles per hour. The world record for an electric train was set by a TGV in 1981. It got up to 236 miles per hour. But that was unusually fast. TGVs in service today regularly reach a high speed of 186 miles per hour.

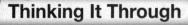

Thinking It Through

1. What was the author's purpose in writing this passage?

   A. to entertain

   B. to inform or teach

   C. to make you feel a certain way

   D. to change the way you think about something

   HINT How do you feel after reading the passage? This passage is interesting, but it is not entertaining. It doesn't change the way you think or feel about trains.

2. How do you know the purpose of the passage?

   A. It gives several facts about bullet trains.

   B. It gives several opinions about bullet trains.

   C. It is written in paragraphs.

   D. It is fun to read.

   HINT While a passage like this might be entertaining, this does not show its purpose. Also, the passage has few opinions.

Lesson Practice

Coached Reading

DIRECTIONS
Read the passage below. While you are reading, look to the Reading Guide for tips.

Aaron Tippin

1   Aaron Tippin is a famous country music singer from Traveler's Rest, South Carolina. He has been singing all of his life. He used to sing on the farm when he was a boy. It kept him busy while he was working.

2   His father was a pilot, and Aaron wanted to be a pilot, too. He learned how to fly and fix planes. He got a job as a private pilot, but he wanted to work for an airline. Then there was a gas shortage. It got too expensive to fly, so there wasn't any work for new pilots. Aaron decided to go to Nashville, Tennessee, to try singing.

3   It took a few years, but he was successful. He wrote and sang his own songs. Some of his songs, such as "Where the Stars and Stripes and the Eagle Fly," are patriotic. Other songs, such as "Her," are love songs. There are even some songs, such as "Mission from Hank," that tell a story.

4   The songs that Aaron writes and sings are really good. If you are a fan of country music, you should listen to some of them. Some of them are fast, and some of them are slow. But they're all enjoyable.

Reading Guide

What feelings or thoughts come to mind while reading? They might be related to the purpose.

Does the last paragraph do something different from the others? There can be more than one purpose in the same piece of writing.

Independent Practice

DIRECTIONS
Use the passage to answer questions 1–4.

1. According to the selection, why did Aaron Tippin write the song "Where the Stars and the Stripes and the Eagle Fly"?

   A. to make people feel sad

   B. to make people feel proud of their country

   C. to teach people about eagles

   D. to explain what stars are

2. What was Aaron Tippin's main purpose in writing the song "Mission from Hank"?

   A. to teach people something

   B. to make people feel romantic

   C. to explain how to write music

   D. to tell a story about someone

3. Which of the following BEST describes the author's purpose for writing paragraph 4?

   A. to persuade

   B. to inform

   C. to entertain

   D. to predict

4. What is the author's MAIN purpose for writing "Aaron Tippin"?

   A. to explain how difficult it is to be a commercial pilot

   B. to teach the lesson that dreams can come true

   C. to tell about the life of a successful country singer

   D. to explain how songs are written

18 Realistic Story Elements

R.2.e, R.3.a

Getting the Idea

A **fact** is something true or real. It can be proven. Passages like newspaper stories and textbook articles use facts. Real-life stories also use facts. They tell you information that is true. **Fiction** is something pretend or make-believe. Fairy tales and other made-up stories are fictional passages. They describe things that did not really happen.

It can be hard to figure out whether a story is fiction or about facts. Sometimes fictional passages are very realistic—they seem like they are true. They may be set in a time or place that seems real. The events may seem like something that could really happen. The characters may remind you of people you really know.

To figure out if a story is fiction, look for something that could not really happen. Study the setting, events, characters, and actions. To figure out if a story is based on facts, look for a sentence or note that says the passage is true.

Read the passage below. Decide whether the passage is fact or fiction. Search for clues that show whether the information is true or pretend. Look for elements that make the passage seem real.

> Heather's cat meowed and meowed. She could tell he was hungry. "I just don't know what to feed you," she said to the cat. "I'm not sure if you would like fish or chicken or something else." The cat looked up at her sharply and said, "I don't care what you feed me, just give it to me NOW!"

This passage is fiction. You can tell it is make-believe because cats cannot really talk. Other than that, though, the story was realistic. There could be a girl named Heather with a cat. That cat might meow if it were hungry. Heather might not be sure about what to feed the cat.

Coached Example

DIRECTIONS
Read this passage and answer the questions that follow.

Ten-year-old Tilly was walking along a crowded beach with her family. Some very strange things started happening. The seawater rushed away from the beach and began bubbling. No one seemed to know what was going on. But Tilly could understand the ocean's "warning." She learned about tsunamis in school. Tsunamis are giant waves. They are very dangerous. Tilly recognized signs that a giant wave was coming. She explained the danger to her parents, and they told everyone else. People quickly left the beach before the giant wave could sweep them away. Thanks to Tilly, not one person on that beach was harmed.

Editor's note: Tilly Smith was in Thailand on December 26th, 2004, the day of the tsunami. The story of her quick thinking is supposed to be true.

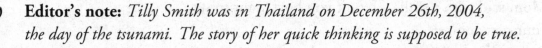

Thinking It Through

1. Which part of the story tells the reader that this event may really have happened?

   A. the events in the story

   B. the setting of the story

   C. the character in the story

   D. the note at the end of the story

   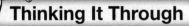 **HINT** A story can be realistic without being real. What part of the story shows that it is about facts, or things that are real and true?

2. Read this sentence from the passage.

   But Tilly could understand the ocean's "warning."

   Why does the author put quotation marks around *warning*?

   A. to tell what someone said about the ocean

   B. to point out a word that the ocean sounds like

   C. to show that oceans cannot really warn humans

   D. to explain that Tilly has a special connection to the ocean

   HINT Usually quotation marks are used to show what someone is saying. Sometimes they are used to show that a word is used in an unusual way.

Lesson Practice

Coached Reading

DIRECTIONS
Read the passage below. While you are reading, look to the Reading Guide for tips.

The Glass Monkey

Reading Guide

1   Kevin and Brian stood quietly in front of the huge grey house. The old wavy glass in the windows seemed to wink at them in the sun. "What are you waiting for?" Mom said with a smile. "Don't you boys want to see your new rooms?"

In real life, people move to new homes all the time.

2   The brothers grinned at each other. Then they raced inside and up the winding staircase. Dad had already painted their names on each door. "In a house this old, your room has got to be haunted!" Kevin teased as he closed the door to his new bedroom. Brian crept nervously into his own new room.

3   Kevin started exploring the sunny bedroom right away. On one tiny shelf he found a note wrapped around a small glass monkey. The note read: *Whoever holds the monkey, do so with care. Should it ever be broken, BEWARE.*

Finding a note like that is strange, but it could happen.

4   Just then, Brian burst in. "I think I saw a ghost in my room!" He cried as he grabbed his older brother's arm. The monkey slipped right out of Kevin's hand. It shattered on the floor! Before either boy could say a word, the shards of glass began swirling together. The glass formed a silver monkey—a real, live one!

There is an event in this paragraph that could never really happen.

Independent Practice

DIRECTIONS
Use the passage to answer questions 1–4.

1. This passage is MOST like a

    A. news story.

    B. fairy tale.

    C. real-life story.

    D. textbook article.

2. Which sentence from the story tells something that could NOT really happen?

    A. "Kevin and Brian stood quietly in front of the huge grey house."

    B. "Dad had already painted their names on each door."

    C. "On one tiny shelf he found a note wrapped around a small glass monkey."

    D. "The glass formed a silver monkey—a real, live one!"

3. Which story element is LEAST realistic in this passage?

    A. the events

    B. the setting

    C. the characters

    D. the character's actions

4. Which paragraph reveals that this passage is fiction?

    A. paragraph 1

    B. paragraph 2

    C. paragraph 3

    D. paragraph 4

19 Important and Unimportant Details

R.3.a

Getting the Idea

A story or article would not make sense without details. When you are reading something, stop and look at the details that support the main idea. Which ones are the most important? Which ones could be left out? Always think to yourself, "Does this detail help me understand the main idea?" If the answer is "no," it is probably not an important detail to remember.

There are many ways to identify the important information in a passage. One way is to ask yourself questions while reading. Read the passage below.

> Dana yawned. Her eyelids felt heavy. It was 11:30. She had to stay awake just a bit longer.

Readers might ask the following questions to better understand this passage: Why does Dana yawn? Why are her eyelids heavy? What is she struggling to stay awake for? The answers to these questions tell you the most important things you should understand about the passage.

Here are a few tips for identifying important details in a passage.

- Look for the names of people and places, as well as dates.

- Look for certain key words and phrases, such as *most important* and *greatest*.

- Look for any headings, bullet points, underlined or bolded words, or information that is set off from the text.

- Look for the main idea of each paragraph you read. Main ideas are most often found in the first or last sentence of a paragraph. Any important details will be related to the main idea.

- Read the introduction and conclusion of a passage. The most important information is usually stated in these sections.

Coached Example

Read this passage and answer the questions that follow.

Jason's mouth was dry. His legs felt heavy. He tried to listen to the words of his instructor, but he was too nervous to concentrate. The hatch to the plane opened and Jason stepped to the edge. This was his first solo jump. He took a deep breath and thought about everything he had learned. He looked once at the ground, ten thousand feet below. Jason's knees went weak for a moment. After taking a deep breath, Jason leapt from the airplane. Less than five minutes later, Jason was safely on the ground and packing up his parachute. He had done it.

Thinking It Through

1. What is one question readers might ask to better understand how Jason feels before jumping?

    A. Why do Jason's knees go weak?

    B. How old is Jason in this story?

    C. Where is Jason's instructor?

    D. What will Jason do after landing?

    HINT Asking questions can help you understand the important information in a story or passage. The correct answer should be related to Jason's emotions.

2. Which detail is the MOST important to understanding what Jason is doing in the passage?

    A. Jason is feeling nervous.

    B. Jason tries to listen to his instructor.

    C. Jason steps to the edge of the plane.

    D. Jason takes a deep breath.

    HINT Three of these answer choices could take place in a number of settings or situations. Only one detail gives information about the activity Jason is doing.

Coached Reading

DIRECTIONS
Read the passage below. While you are reading, look to the Reading Guide for tips.

To Protect and Serve

Reading Guide

1   Officer Sharon Lewis joined the police force at the age of 22. She wanted to help people. On Friday night, she helped one family a great deal.

2   Officer Lewis was on patrol in Forest Park. It was 8:00. As she turned onto Oak Street, she noticed something strange. She slowed down.

Where and when does this passage take place?

3   Officer Lewis saw a man. He was dressed entirely in black and wearing a ski mask. The man crept outside of a house on Oak Street. Officer Lewis was concerned. After all, it was June. It was also 75 degrees outside. Obviously, he was up to no good.

What question might readers ask to better understand the situation in this paragraph?

4   Officer Lewis got out of her car. She yelled for the man to stop what he was doing. Right away, the man took off running. The man's sneakers squeaked on the street. He ran toward the 9th Street playground, and Officer Lewis chased him.

5   She shouted for the man to stop, but he kept running. Officer Lewis refused to give up. Her legs burned, and her lungs gasped for air. Still, she kept the man in her sights. When he tried to run past DeSalvo's grocery store, Officer Lewis caught up to and tackled him.

6   After handcuffing the man, Officer Lewis learned that he was planning to break into the Jasper family's home. The family was on vacation in Florida. They visited their relatives there every year. The thief would have been able to steal all of their valuables. When they learned of Officer Lewis's brave actions, the Jaspers were very relieved and thankful.

Which events are most important to the plot of the story?

Independent Practice

DIRECTIONS
Use the passage to answer questions 1–4.

1. Where does Officer Lewis first see the man in the ski mask?

   A. at the 9th Street playground

   B. at the police station

   C. in front of DeSalvo's grocery store

   D. in front of a house on Oak Street

2. Which of these details is MOST important to the story?

   A. Sharon Lewis became a police officer when she was 22.

   B. The man in the ski mask was planning to rob the Jaspers' house.

   C. The Jasper family was thankful for Office Lewis' actions.

   D. The man's sneakers squeaked as he ran from Officer Lewis.

3. Which detail shows that Officer Lewis is a good police officer?

   A. She chases the man even though she is out of breath.

   B. She joined the police at a very young age.

   C. She drives around Forest Park when she is on patrol.

   D. She knows her way around the neighborhood.

4. Which of these details is NOT important to the story?

   A. Officer Lewis sees a man in a ski mask.

   B. The man runs away from Officer Lewis.

   C. Officer Lewis tackles and handcuffs the thief.

   D. The Jasper family goes to Florida every year.

20 Fact, Opinion, and Exaggeration

Getting the Idea

Do you know what the difference is between a fact and an opinion? A **fact** is a claim that is always true for everyone. You can prove a fact. An opinion is a belief. An **opinion** might be true for one person, but not for another. You cannot prove an opinion. To figure out whether something is a fact or an opinion, ask yourself if it is always true for everyone.

Read these sentences about chocolate. Look for facts and opinions.

> Chocolate flavoring comes from cocoa beans. Chocolate flavoring is used in many things, such as cakes, cookies, and ice cream. Chocolate has a better flavor than vanilla. Chocolate frosting makes cakes taste delicious.

The first two sentences about chocolate are facts. They can be checked. You can look in an encyclopedia or ask a chocolate maker to prove them. The information is always true, no matter who says it.

The last two sentences tell the author's opinion. What do you think when you read these statements? You might agree with them, or you might not. Even if some people agree, not everyone will.

Authors may also use exaggeration in their writing. An **exaggeration** is a statement that is not entirely true. It bends the truth to prove a point. For example, the sentence, "It was a thousand degrees outside," is an exaggeration. It wasn't *really* a thousand degrees—no one could survive in that heat! The author stretches the truth to help the reader understand that the temperature was uncomfortably hot.

Coached Example

DIRECTIONS
Read this passage and answer the questions that follow.

In some places in the United States, there is very little change in the weather as the seasons change. Those places are not as interesting as the Northeast. In the Northeast, the weather is different in each season.

Changes in temperature bring changes in scenery. In the fall, leafy trees are at their most beautiful. Their orange, yellow, gold, and red colors can be seen from September through October. After a few weeks, the leaves die and fall off.

The bare trees look ugly all winter, until spring comes along. Spring in the Northeast is a time of green buds and shoots. The warmer weather is a relief after the cold winter. Some early flowers start to bloom, bringing spots of color to a mostly brown landscape. Summer, of course, is the time when many plants bloom. For the short growing season, flowers burst open in many gardens. Bright flowers can always make you smile.

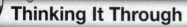 **Thinking It Through**

1. Which of the following is a fact?

   A. "In the fall, leafy trees are at their most beautiful."

   B. "The bare trees look ugly all winter, until spring comes along."

   C. "In the Northeast, the weather is different in each season."

   D. "Bright flowers can always make you smile."

   HINT Remember that a fact is a statement that can be proven. *Beautiful, ugly,* and *always* are all words that show opinions.

2. Which of the following is an opinion?

   A. "Those places are not as interesting as the Northeast."

   B. "In some places in the United States, there is very little change in the weather as the seasons change."

   C. "Changes in temperature bring changes in scenery."

   D. "After a few weeks, the leaves die and fall off."

   HINT Remember that an opinion tells what someone thinks. Which of these sentences shows a personal belief?

Lesson Practice

Coached Reading

DIRECTIONS
Read the passage below. While you are reading, look to the
Reading Guide for tips.

Hail to the Chief!

1   Any time the president comes into the room for an
official matter, a certain song is played. There are no
words to the song. It is only a tune. The name of this
tune is "Hail to the Chief."

2   This tradition started in the mid-1800s. The president
at the time was a man named James K. Polk. Polk was
a terribly short man. He was also very plain looking.
When he came into a room, nobody noticed he was
there. This upset his wife, Sarah. She decided to do
something about it.

3   Sarah talked to the head of the Marine band. She
told him, "I want you to play something whenever the
president enters the room."

4   "What shall I play?" the bandleader asked.

5   "A distinguished song would be best," she replied.

6   The bandleader told the musicians to play an old
Scottish song. The song was called "Hail to the Chief."
Whenever Polk came into a room, the music played.
That music was a signal that it was time to get up to see
the president.

7   Playing "Hail to the Chief" when the president
entered quickly became a tradition. Every president
since then has had the song played for important
occasions. It is a great song that symbolizes
the president.

Reading Guide

Is it a fact that there are no
words to the song? Can it
be proved?

Do you think it is true that
nobody noticed James
Polk? It is likely that at
least one person would
have noticed the president.

Words like *great* and *best*
often show opinions.

Independent Practice

DIRECTIONS
Use the passage to questions 1–4.

1. Which of the following is an opinion?

   A. "Sarah talked to the head of the Marine band."

   B. "There are no words to the song."

   C. "The name of this tune is 'Hail to the Chief.'"

   D. "It is a great song that symbolizes the president."

2. Which of the following is a fact?

   A. "This tradition started in the mid-1800s."

   B. "Polk was a terribly short man."

   C. "He was also very plain looking."

   D. "A distinguished song would be best. . . ."

3. Read this sentence from the passage.

   The president at the time was a man names James K. Polk.

   If you wanted to prove this fact, which would be the BEST source to use?

   A. a current newspaper

   B. a history textbook

   C. a short story

   D. an advertisement

4. Read this sentence from the passage.

   When he came into a room, nobody noticed he was there.

   This sentence is an exaggeration because it

   A. shows a personal belief.

   B. can be supported by proof.

   C. happened too long ago to be proved true.

   D. stretches the truth to prove a point.

3 Review

Directions
Read this story. Then answer questions 1 through 6.

The Tongue-Cut Sparrow

a Japanese folktale

There once lived a couple who had no children. They had no money, so they had a lot of work to do. The man's only happiness was a little sparrow. Day after day, the bird lifted the man's spirits with its sweet singing. It made the sparrow happy to see the man smile.

One morning, while the man was out cutting wood, his wife set out to do some laundry. Before long, the sparrow flew into the sheets the woman had hung out to dry.

"How could you?" the woman asked the little bird angrily. Without waiting for a reply, she reached for the bird and cut his tongue—swiftly. Shocked more than hurt, the little bird flew off.

That night, when the man returned, his wife told him about the sparrow. "Can you believe the nerve of that bird?" she asked as she told her story. The man didn't hesitate. He didn't even take time to reply. With just a dark look at his wife, he set off to find the little bird.

Into the woods, the man journeyed. Soon, the trees grew thick. And the woods grew dark. The man, already upset, grew forlorn. He was worried about his friend—worried he wouldn't find him. "Where are you, little friend?" the man called. "I hope you're not too hurt."

Just then, the man heard a few notes of a song. It was the sparrow, and he was singing!

"Ah!" the man cried. "There you are!" He smiled broadly as the sparrow flew to him.

"I'm fine," the sparrow chirped, "but touched by your kindness. To thank you, I'd like to give you something."

"Just more songs," the man said. "Those make my heart happy."

"No, here," the little bird insisted, offering two baskets. "I'll give you a choice: one light, one heavy."

The man had a long trip home, so his choice was easy. "Thank you, little bird," he said. "I'll take the one that's light. If nothing else, it'll be less to carry."

"Very well," smiled the bird. "Then I give it to you on one condition: Just don't open it until you're home."

Nodding happily, the man set off. His wife greeted him with wide eyes. For when the man removed the basket's lid, jewels of all kinds sparkled inside.

The woman's eyes grew wider still. "I'm going back for the heavy basket!" she cried.

When she found the sparrow, he smiled slyly. "Here's my chance to get even," he thought. So, again, the sparrow made his offer: take the basket, but wait to open it. The woman, though, went just a few steps before she looked inside. There, more things gleamed and glistened. The woman happily reached inside, but quickly pulled back. For the basket didn't hold jewels—it held snakes!

The woman ran the rest of the way home, leaving the basket far behind. At home, she sobbed when she saw her husband. "If only I'd been happy with the first basket," she cried.

Go On

1 Why did the author **most likely** write this story?

    A to share ideas about how to get rich

    B to convince readers to be kind to birds

    C to entertain readers with a story about a sparrow

    D to explain the importance of never hurting animals

2 This story is **most** like a

    A fairy tale

    B news story

    C real-life story

    D textbook article

3 Which of these details is **most** important to the story?

    A where the sparrow flies away to

    B what chore the sparrow disturbed

    C why the wife seeks out the sparrow

    D that the man and his wife have no children

4 Which sentence from the story tells something that could **not** really happen?

    A "The woman ran the rest of the way home, leaving the basket far behind."

    B "Day after day, the bird lifted the man's spirits with its sweet singing."

    C "One morning, while the man was out cutting wood, his wife set out to do some laundry."

    D "So, again, the sparrow made his offer: take the basket, but wait to open it."

5 Which part of the story tells the reader that this story could **not** really have happened?

    A the title of the story

    B the wife's actions

    C the way the man cares for the sparrow

    D the way the sparrow smiles and speaks

6 Why does the author **most likely** include the information about how poor the man and his wife are?

    A to explain why the wife has such a short temper

    B to show that the sparrow's gift means a lot to the man

    C to explain how the sparrow could be so friendly

    D to show how much the man likes the sparrow's singing

Go On

What's So Bad About Bats?

by Anne Mueller

Many people think that bats are creepy and bad. This reputation is undeserved. Bats are actually wonderful creatures. They are no more dangerous than house flies. People may have these wrong ideas because bats are not familiar to most of us. Many people rarely see bats in person. But in photos, they can look frightening. Their lips are often curled back, showing their teeth. Bats only do this when they sense danger, such as when someone comes close to take a picture.

Bats live in most parts of the world. There are about 900 kinds of bats. Many are small, though each species looks different from the others. They are the only mammals that can truly fly. (Flying squirrels glide rather than fly.)

A Tasty Diet

If insects bug you, enjoy this fact: most bats eat insects, sometimes in very large amounts. Some small bats can eat hundreds, or even thousands, of insects in one night. Bats are the best exterminators in the world!

> exterminator = someone who kills bugs

Most bats eat larger insects such as moths, but will also eat smaller insects such as flies and mosquitoes. Some bats eat ripe fruit, nectar, small fish, frogs, birds, or rodents. Some bats even eat other bats!

Blind as a Bat

All bats *can* see. But some also are able to use sounds to find their way in the dark. These bats make special noises. Then they listen for sounds that bounce back from things around them. The bats can "see" the sounds just as people can see pictures from light reflected into their eyes.

In this way, bats are able to escape dangers and catch food in complete darkness. This lets them hunt and feed at night, and sleep during the day.

Just Hanging Around

It's true: when sleeping or just resting, bats hang upside down. This may seem strange, but their bodies allow them to do this. This ability lets bats roost in places where other animals cannot. These places include the ceilings of caves and the rafters of old buildings. Caves can be very popular with bats. A large cave in Texas has twenty million bats living in it.

Bat Motels

Sometimes people build bat houses hoping to attract bats to their yards and give them a safe place to live. Bats will often move into the bat houses unless some other animals or insects take them over first. If you would like to help out a family of bats, look for library books or websites that tell how to build a bat house and where to place it.

Your new bat friends will eat up unwanted pests in your yard, like bugs and rodents. Perhaps you'll even get a close-up glimpse of them when the sun hangs low in the sky. You will surely see that these wonderful creatures are nothing to be afraid of. These furry flying mammals should be welcomed and celebrated!

7 Why does the author **most likely** include the information about bat's vision?

   A to show how bats listen instead of seeing

   B to explain how bats can hunt during the day

   C to explain why bats do not bump into things

   D to show that the belief that bats are blind is false

8 This passage is **most** like

   A a fairy tale

   B realistic fiction

   C a textbook article

   D a real-life story

Go On

9 The author **most likely** wrote this passage in order to

A entertain readers with a story about bats

B teach readers how to keep bats as pets

C show readers that bats are better than insects

D inform readers that bats are interesting and not scary

10 Which sentence from the passage is an **opinion**?

A "Bats are actually wonderful creatures."

B "Many people rarely see bats in person."

C "There are about 900 kinds of bats."

D "Some bats even eat other bats!"

11 Which of these details is **least** important to the passage?

A what bats like to eat

B how bats can see in the dark

C what people do to attract bats

D how insects bother some people

12 Read this sentence from the passage.

Bats are the best exterminators in the world!

Why is this sentence an exaggeration?

A It can be supported by proof.

B It stretches the truth to prove a point.

C It gives a personal opinion.

D It is based on ideas that are not real.

STOP

CHAPTER

4 Listening

21 Take Notes

Getting the Idea

In this chapter, you will practice your listening skills. Unlike other passages, you may not have the listening passage written down in front of you. So, you may not be able to look back at the passage when you are answering questions about it.

Don't worry! You do not have to remember everything the teacher reads. You can write down notes about the passage. Your notes will help you remember the most important details from the passage.

The teacher will not be reading very fast, but you will not have time to write down everything. There are a few important things you should listen for, and make sure to write in your notes. This is the kind of information that you will most likely be asked about later.

- Write down any problems in the story and how they are solved. Also note the reasons for character actions.

- Write down the main events in the story, and the order they happen in. Also note who the events happen to and where they take place.

- Write down how the main character changes from the beginning of the story to the end. Note how the character's actions, feelings, or thoughts change.

Don't forget to keep listening as you write. You do not want to miss important information while you are writing a note.

It is important to remember that your notes will not be graded. So, you do not have to worry about writing in complete sentences, using your neatest handwriting, or checking your spelling or grammar.

Your notes are only for you. It is only important that you be able to read and understand the notes you have made.

Coached Example

DIRECTIONS
Your teacher will read this passage aloud to you. You may take notes on a separate sheet of paper. Answer the questions that follow.

Ruth Mosko was the child of poor Polish immigrants. She was the youngest of ten children. Her life was not easy. Her mother was so sick that Ruth was raised by an older sister. When Ruth was 19 years old, she left her home in Denver for a vacation to Hollywood. She never came back. Her high school sweetheart followed her to California and married her. Her name became Ruth Handler.

Ruth worked hard and started a business with her husband. Fifteen years later Ruth invented a doll, which she called Barbie. She named the doll after her daughter, Barbara. She hoped girls could use the doll to act out their dreams. Barbie was a success, and Ruth's business grew much larger. Ruth became a very wealthy woman.

Thinking It Through

1. How does Ruth change from the beginning of the passage to the end?

   A. She is sick, and then she is healthy.

   B. She is unhappy, and then she is happy.

   C. She is poor, and then she becomes rich.

   D. She is lazy, and then becomes hard working.

   HINT Remember, it is important to take notes on how the main character changes throughout a passage. Notice how Ruth is described at the beginning of the passage. Then, think about how she is described at the end.

2. At the end of the passage, why does Ruth's business grow?

   A. Ruth moves to Hollywood.

   B. Ruth invents a very popular doll.

   C. Ruth and her husband work hard.

   D. Ruth has a daughter named Barbara.

   HINT This question asks you for a reason why something happened. What changes in Ruth's life before her company starts growing larger?

Lesson Practice

Coached Listening

DIRECTIONS

You are going to listen to a story called "Andy's Ice House." You will listen to the story twice. The first time you hear the story, listen carefully but do not take notes. As you listen to the story the second time, use the space below to take notes. While you are taking notes, look to the Listening Guide for tips.

Notes

Listening Guide

Shorten character names to help you write faster. For example, instead of writing "Andy" just write "A."

Notice what Andy thinks and says when he first discovers the snow is icy.

Think about how Andy's feelings about the icy snow have changed. What causes him to feel differently?

Independent Practice

DIRECTIONS
Use your notes about the passage to help you answer questions 1–4.

1. In the story, what problem does Andy have?

   A. The snow is not soft.

   B. The snow is not slippery.

   C. There is not enough snow.

   D. He wears the wrong boots.

2. What are two plans Andy has for playing in the snow at the beginning of the story?

   A. making a snowman and going sledding

   B. making an ice house and going sledding

   C. making a snowman and going ice skating

   D. making snow angels and having a snowball fight

3. What causes Andy's feelings about the icy snow to change?

   A. He does not fall on it.

   B. He gets to go sledding.

   C. He talks to his mother about it.

   D. He learns to build things with it.

4. How does Andy feel at the end of the story?

   A. eager

   B. angry

   C. proud

   D. disappointed

22 Organize Information

Getting the Idea

After reading or listening to a passage, you may be asked to organize information from the passage. Some questions will tell you to put the information into a graphic organizer. **Graphic organizers** help arrange and display information.

You learned about different types of graphic organizers in Lesson 9. Two types of graphic organizers you may be asked to fill in are charts and sequence charts, like the ones shown below. The examples show you the kind of information you will be given, and the kind of information you may be asked to fill in.

CHART

Subject from passage
1) A detail about subject
2) A detail about subject
3) A detail about subject

SEQUENCE CHART

The first event or step from the passage

↓

The second event or step from the passage

↓

The third event or step from the passage

↓

The last event or step from the passage

As you know, charts show information in rows and columns. Sequence charts are used to show the order of events that take place in a passage. They also show how one event leads to another. If you come across a graphic organizer on a test, it will be based on ideas from the passage you have just read. Some of the details may also be filled in for you, but you must complete the rest of the graphic organizer. The information you write must be based on the passage.

Coached Example

DIRECTIONS

Your teacher will read this passage aloud to you. You may take notes on a separate sheet of paper. Answer the question that follows.

Getting a plant to grow from a seed can be difficult. There are other ways to grow your own plant. One of the easiest ways is through plant clippings. A plant clipping is a branch from another plant. It should include a stem and leaves.

First, fill a small clear jar with water. Then put the bottom of the clipping into the water. Make sure the leaves are above the water. Place the clipping near a window for sunlight. After a week or two, you should see little roots growing out of the stem and into the water. Once the whole jar is filled with roots, it is time to put your plant in soil.

Thinking It Through

1. The chart below shows what to do when growing a plant from a clipping. Complete the chart with details from the passage.

HOW TO GROW A PLANT FROM A CLIPPING

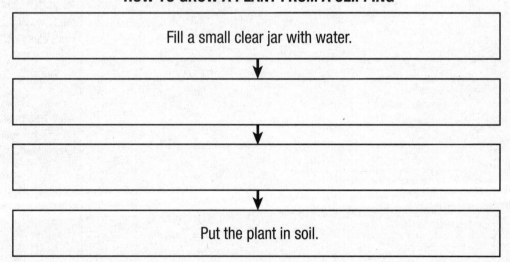

HINT The top box displays the first step or thing you should do. What does the passage say to do next? You must write that information in the first blank box. What does it tell you to do after that? You must write that information in the second blank box.

Lesson Practice

Coached Listening

DIRECTIONS

You are going to listen to a story called "The Royal Storyteller." You will listen to the story twice. The first time you hear the story, listen carefully but do not take notes. As you listen to the story the second time, use the space below to take notes. While you are taking notes, look to the Listening Guide for tips.

Notes

_____

_____

_____

_____

_____

_____

_____

_____

_____

_____

_____

_____

Listening Guide

The narrator's name is Spider. Notice how Spider first began telling stories.

Try to remember what kind of stories Spider tells for each trial. Also notice the types of tales other storytellers use.

What type of stories do the prince, the queen, and the king seem to like?

Independent Practice

DIRECTIONS
Use your notes about the passage to help you answer questions 1–2.

1. Using information from the story, complete the chart below with who listens to the story in each trial and what story Spider told them.

Who Listens to the Story in Each Trial	What Story Spider Told Them
Trial 1: the prince	an exciting adventure about a prince
Trial 2:	
Trial 3:	

2. The chart below shows what happens in the story. Complete the chart with details from the story.

WHAT HAPPENS IN THIS STORY

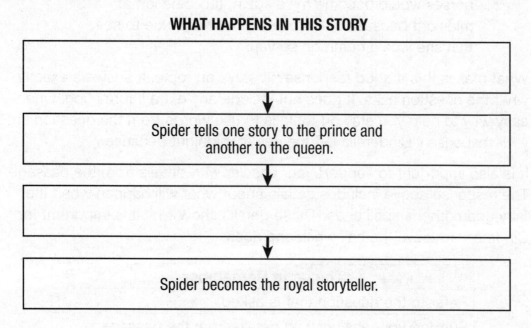

Spider tells one story to the prince and another to the queen.

Spider becomes the royal storyteller.

23 Write a Short Response

Getting the Idea

A short-response question asks the reader to respond to a passage in his or her own words. When you answer a short-response question, you need to show how well you understand the passage in a few sentences.

Short-response questions usually ask something specific about the passage. A short-response question about the story of Cinderella might be, "Why did Cinderella leave the ball at midnight? Use details from the story to support your answer." Read this response:

> Cinderella left the ball at midnight because that is when the fairy godmother's spell ended. Cinderella's beautiful gown would soon change back into her normal clothes. Her coach would also turn back into a pumpkin. The horses would become mice again, too. She left at midnight because she did not want the prince to see that she was a common servant.

What makes this a good response? It stays on topic. It answers exactly what the question asks. It does not include any extra information. One easy way to help you stay on topic is to use words from the question in your response ("Cinderella left the ball at midnight because . . .").

It is also important to support your answer with details from the passage. The response above includes details about what will happen when the fairy godmother's spell ends. Those details show why it is important for Cinderella to leave the ball when she does.

Things to Remember
Refer to the question that is asked.
Support your answer with details from the passage.
Write in complete sentences.
Use proper grammar and spelling.
Use neat handwriting.

Coached Example

DIRECTIONS
Your teacher will read this passage aloud to you. You make take notes on a separate sheet of paper. Answer the questions that follow.

The Civil War was a war between the northern states and the southern states. The battles in this war were often fierce. When the war first broke out, there was a big battle called the First Battle of Bull Run. The McLean family farm was near this battlefield. They saw a lot of soldiers from both sides. They could hear and see the fighting. They decided to move away to some place safer.

The McLeans moved to a quiet place called Appomattox Court House. They felt happier and safer there. A few years later, they were affected by the war again. Just as their old farm had been the scene of the beginning of the war, their house was where it ended. The two generals who got together to agree to end the war met in the McLean house. The family just couldn't get away from that war.

Thinking It Through

1. Why did the McLean family move? Use details from the passage to support your answer.

   _____

   _____

   _____

   _____

   _____

   HINT Think about what is happening at the beginning of the passage.

2. How was the McLean's second home like their first home? Use details from the passage to support your answer.

   _____

   _____

   _____

   _____

   _____

   HINT The McLean family had the same problem at each of their homes. What was it?

Lesson Practice

Coached Listening

DIRECTIONS

You are going to listen to an article called "Becoming a Monster." You will listen to the article twice. The first time you hear the article, listen carefully but do not take notes. As you listen to the article the second time, use the space below to take notes. While you are taking notes, look to the Listening Guide for tips.

Notes

Listening Guide

What is the movie *Frankenstein* based on?

Why did actors turn down the role of the monster?

How did Boris Karloff become a big star?

Independent Practice

DIRECTIONS
Use your notes about the passage to help you answer questions 1–3.

1. Explain why many famous actors did not want to play the role of the monster.
   Use details from the passage to support your answer.

   _____

   _____

   _____

2. How did Boris Karloff prepare for the role of the monster in Frankenstein?
   Use details from the passage to support your answer.

   _____

   _____

   _____

   _____

3. What did Boris Karloff do after he made Frankenstein? Use details from the passage
   to support your answer.

   _____

   _____

   _____

   _____

4 Review

***D**irections*
You are going to listen to a story called "The Sound of Thunder." Then you will answer questions 1 through 4 about the story.

You will listen to the story twice. The first time you hear the story, listen carefully but do not take notes. As you listen to the story the second time, you may want to take notes. Use the space below and on the next page for your notes. You may use these notes to answer the questions that follow. Your notes on these pages will NOT count toward your Chapter Review score.

Notes

Notes

STOP

1 Complete the chart below with **three** details from the story that show how Tanu helps Tushar.

How Tanu Helps Tushar
1)
2)
3)

2 In the story, what is the problem that other animals have with Tushar? Does Tushar think it is a problem? Use details from the story to support your answer.

_____

_____

_____

_____

_____

_____

3 Tushar's voice affects different people and animals in different ways. Complete the chart below to show how each character responds to Tushar's voice.

Part of Story	The Effect of Tushar's Voice
Beginning of story	Ashwin thinks there is thunder, and sends his children inside.
Middle of story	
End of story	

4 Below are two words that describe Tanu. Circle the **one** that best describes her.

kind   understanding

Give two examples from the story to support your choice.

1. _____

_____

_____

2. _____

_____

_____

STOP

Directions

You are going to listen to a story called "Rescue in the Park." Then you will answer questions 5 through 8 about the story.

You will listen to the story twice. The first time you hear the story, listen carefully but do not take notes. As you listen to the story the second time, you may want to take notes. Use the space below and on the next page for your notes. You may use these notes to answer the questions that follow. Your notes on these pages will NOT count toward your Chapter Review score.

Notes

Notes

STOP

5 How does Mrs. O'Malley feel at the beginning of the story? Why does she feel this way? Use details from the story to support your answer.

_____

_____

_____

_____

_____

6 The chart below shows what happens in the story. Complete the chart with details from the story.

WHAT HAPPENS IN THIS STORY

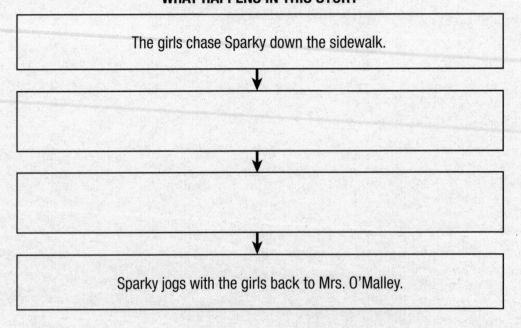

The girls chase Sparky down the sidewalk.

↓

↓

↓

Sparky jogs with the girls back to Mrs. O'Malley.

7 At the end of the story, why does everyone head back to the apartment building? Use details from the story to support your answer.

_____

_____

_____

_____

_____

8 The characters in the story try to get Sparky to come back in different ways. Complete the chart below to show how the characters try to catch Sparky.

Who Tries to Catch Sparky	Way of Trying to Catch Sparky

STOP

CHAPTER

5 Writing

24 Meaning

Getting the Idea

Sometimes, you will be asked to write a long response to a question that is based on a passage you have listened to or read. These questions are called extended-response questions. They have more than one part. It is very important to answer every part of the question.

Most extended-response questions are not simply about information in the passage. They are about the meanings behind the information. You need to look for clues in the passage details to figure out these meanings. These details should support the theme. The **theme** of a passage is a lesson that the passage teaches.

The author does not usually point out the theme directly. For example, in the well-known story "The Boy Who Cried Wolf," the theme is not about shepherd boys or wolves. It is about lies and the harm they do.

Some questions may ask you to make connections between two passages. Let's read the passage below. Think about its theme, and how it connects to the story "The Boy Who Cried Wolf."

> Daryl looked down at his grade. It was another F. He had failing grades in math all year. He managed to hide it from his parents, but the lies were getting harder to tell. Later that night, all of Daryl's lies fell apart. "Daryl, I just got off the phone with your math teacher," Daryl's mother said with a frown. "I wish you had been honest with me. I could have gotten you a tutor, or helped more with your homework. Now you're going to have to go to summer school and miss going to camp." Daryl was in tears.

A common idea shared by the two stories is telling lies. But you can make even more connections between the two stories. In both stories, the boy's lies had terrible outcomes that could have been avoided if each boy had told the truth. Also, the boys in both stories betrayed the trust of people that could have helped them.

Coached Example

Read this passage and answer the question that follows. Write your answer on a separate sheet of paper.

Maggy Macaw squawked from the top of a very tall tree. "Lena, come taste this delicious fruit!" Lena Lemur just looked up nervously at the canopy far above.

Manny Monkey and Sandra Sloth overheard the macaw. Manny ascended quickly, swinging from branch to branch. Sandra slowly climbed up the giant trunk. "Hurry up!" Manny shouted from the top of the tree. "This fruit is unbelievable!"

Other animals made their way to the treetop to see what all the fuss was about. Lena looked up longingly. She knew how to climb trees, but her fear of great heights held her back.

Finally, Lena took a deep breath and scampered up the enormous tree. When she reached the top, she found Sandra licking her paws. "I made it just in time," the sloth said happily. "There was only one fruit left, but it was certainly worth the climb."

Thinking It Through

Think about Lena Lemur from this story. What keeps her from climbing up the tree right away? What happens because she waits? What lesson can she learn from her mistake? Use details from the story to support your answer.

In your answer, be sure to

- explain what keeps Lena from climbing up the tree right away
- tell what happens as a result
- explain what lesson Lena can learn from her mistake
- use details from the story to support your answer

HINT This story is not about moving slow or fast. The fast monkey and even the slow sloth got to enjoy the special fruit. What kept Lena from enjoying the fruit with the rest of the animals? The answer to this question reveals the main message, or theme, of the passage.

Lesson Practice

Coached Reading

DIRECTIONS
Read the passage below. While you are reading, look to the
Reading Guide for tips.

Bringing Joy

1   Long ago, a small village sat alone at the edge of a
cold gray ocean. It had been a hard winter for the village.
The village leaders decided to bring everyone some cheer.
"We should have a contest with a grand reward," one of
the leaders suggested.

2   So a contest was planned. The village leaders gathered
together riches and food. The stack was higher than the
tallest man in the village.

3   "Any person who can get over this stack without
knocking anything down will win the whole pile," the
leaders declared.

4   Almost every villager tried to leap over the stack and
failed. People were even gloomier than before. The village
leaders feared they had made the challenge, and the
reward, too great.

5   Then a few orphan children stepped up to the stack.
Four of the orphans held a blanket in front of the pile.
A tiny orphan girl got onto the blanket and began
jumping. She bounced higher and higher, until she
bounced right over the top of the pile.

6   Everyone rejoiced when the riches were given to the
ones who needed it the most.

Reading Guide

It has been a difficult winter, and the village leaders are making plans to cheer up people. How do you think the villagers are feeling?

When everyone is competing for their own benefit, no one is happy.

The theme, or lesson, of the story is revealed in the last paragraph. Notice how the villagers feel, and why.

Independent Practice

DIRECTIONS
Use the passage to answer the extended-response question. As you write, pay close attention to meaning and theme. You may continue your answer on a separate sheet of paper if you run out of room below.

> The villagers' feelings change in the story. How do they feel at the beginning of the story? How do they feel during the contest? How do they feel at the end of the story? What causes their feelings to change? Use details from the story to support your answer.
>
> In your answer, be sure to include
>
> • how the villagers feel at the beginning of the story
> • how the villagers feel during the contest
> • how the villagers feel at the end of the story
> • what causes the villagers' feelings to change
> • details from the story to support your answer

_____

_____

_____

_____

_____

_____

_____

25 Development

Getting the Idea

When you answer an extended-response question, you need to support your answer with details from the passage. As you know, the **main idea** is what a story or article is mostly about. Your response should also have a main idea.

To identify your main idea, think about what the question asks. For example, an extended-response question about a story might ask, "How does Katie save her kitten from the tree?" The main idea of your response should be "how Katie saves her kitten from the tree."

Details give more information about the main idea. They help the reader understand the main idea and add interest to your writing. To add details, ask yourself questions about the passage:

- Where did this happen?
- When did it happen?
- Why did it happen?
- How did it happen?

When writing an extended response, first state your main idea. Then add details from the passage to support the main idea. Try to choose details that are both important and interesting. Use details to explain each of your points.

Study these two summaries of a passage about eagles. See how the second one uses strong details that support the main idea.

Weak Main Idea and Details	Strong Main Idea and Details
The eagle is very bold and a little mean. It is a large, strong bird. It has a sharp beak and claws. There are many different types of eagles. Many eagles eat fish. Eagles often steal fish from other birds.	The eagle is to birds what the lion is to mammals. The eagle is a large, strong bird. It is also bold, daring, and a little mean. Smaller birds are afraid of its sharp beak and claws. The eagle often steals fish from other birds.

Coached Example

DIRECTIONS

Read this passage and answer the question that follows. Write your answer on a separate sheet of paper.

The camel is an amazing animal that can carry its food and water on long trips. It can hold food in its hump. It stores water in its stomach.

There are two kinds of camels. The Dromedary has one hump on its back. The Bactrian has two humps. The Dromedary is the most common kind of camel. It is smaller than the Bactrian camel. It is also faster. It is from the Arabian desert. It now lives all over North Africa, Arabia, Syria, and Persia. The Bactrian camel lives in the middle of Asia. It is bigger and slower than the Dromedary camel.

All camels are very smart. They are also loyal. They can carry hundreds of pounds on their backs. They can get along in dry places because they do not need much food or water.

Thinking It Through

How are Dromedary and Bactrian camels **alike**? How are they **different**? Compare and contrast the two camels mentioned in the passage. Use details from the passage to support your answer.

In your answer, be sure to include

- how the two camels are **alike**
- how the two camels are **different**
- details from the passage to support your answer

HINT   Planning your response before you begin writing can help you develop your ideas. You can use a graphic organizer to arrange the details you want to use in your answer. You can also make an outline. An outline is a list of the information you want to include in each paragraph.

Lesson Practice

Coached Reading

DIRECTIONS
Read the passage below. While you are reading, look to the Reading Guide for tips.

An Imprint of the Past

Reading Guide

1   Somewhere at this very moment, you can surely find a scientist carefully digging in a pit. You might even see that scientist pick up a rock from that pit. The scientist studies it very carefully. If you go in for a closer look, you can study the rock yourself. You will probably see an imprint in the rock. It might be in the shape of a plant. Or, it could be a footprint or a tooth from an animal. No matter what the impression is, there is one thing you can be sure of—this is an imprint of the distant past.

Read the descriptions of the imprints carefully. Can you picture what is being described?

2   When imprints of ancient plants and animals are left in rock, they are called fossils. Certain scientists study fossils. They reveal a lot about Earth's past. They show us what kind of plants and animals used to live on our planet. They can also help scientists figure out when and why some of those living things disappeared.

Notice what fossils can reveal about living things.

3   Fossils can also give us clues about how the face of Earth has changed. For example, fossils found in Death Valley revealed some very big changes. Death Valley is a desert in California and Nevada. So, you can imagine how surprised scientists must have been when they found fossils of fish and seashells there. These fossils show us that this barren desert was once a shallow ocean filled with sea life.

A desert and an ocean are two very different habitats. This area has changed a lot.

Independent Practice

DIRECTIONS

Use the passage to answer the extended-response question. As you write, pay close attention to developing and supporting your ideas. You may continue your answer on a separate sheet of paper if you run out of room below.

Think about the fossils scientists found in Death Valley. What do they reveal about the area? What do they reveal about things that lived there long ago? How has Death Valley changed? Use details from the passage to support your answer.

In your answer, be sure to include

• what the fossils reveal about Death Valley
• what the fossils reveal about things that lived in Death Valley
• how Death Valley has changed
• details from the passage to support your answer

_____

_____

_____

_____

_____

_____

_____

_____

26 Organization

Getting the Idea

A good answer to an extended-response question must be well organized. This means that you should write your ideas in an order that makes sense. Every time you write, you need to focus on one big idea, or topic. Your **topic sentence** should clearly state what you are going to write about. It comes at the beginning of your response.

After your topic sentence, you should not introduce any different ideas. The facts, examples, and stories used should be about the main topic. Look at these examples.

Weak Organization	Strong Organization
The third grade class did a survey to find out how students travel to school. We found that students travel to school in different ways. Some students travel to school by bus. The students who travel by bus seem to like it. Sometimes it's hard to ride the bus, though. If you miss it, you'll be late for school. But it's fun to read or look out the window on a bus.	The third grade class did a survey to find out how students travel to school. We found that students travel to school by bus, by car, on bicycles, or by walking. The largest number of students travel to school by bus. We found that 72 of the 150 students we talked to come to school by bus. So, about half of the students we talked to ride the bus.

In the first example, the writer does not stay on topic. The second example is much stronger. The writer stays focused on the main topic, which is the survey.

Transition words will also help you organize your writing. They are words that come between ideas. *First*, *next*, *then*, *however*, *after*, and *finally* are examples of transitions. Transitions connect ideas so that the writing flows smoothly from one idea to the next.

Coached Example

DIRECTIONS

Read this passage and answer the question that follows. Write your answer on a separate sheet of paper.

Many years ago, there were very few public schools in the United States. Wealthy parents sent their children to private schools. A few poor children went to charity schools.

The rich and poor children never met each other because they did not go to the same schools. At that time most children did not go to school at all. As a result, many people could not read, write, or do much math.

In the 1800s, this began to change. People then said that all children should be educated. Many states began to offer free public schools. These new schools usually just had one teacher. Children of all ages sat in one room and learned together. They were taught to read, write, and do math.

Although the first schools were small, they were a start. Today all children in America have the right to go to free public schools.

Thinking It Through

How have public schools in the United States changed? Describe how schools in the United State once were. Then describe what schools are like today. Use details from the passage to support your answer.

In your answer, be sure to include

• how U.S. schools used to be

• what U.S. schools are like today

• details from the passage to support your answer

HINT Remember to begin your response with a topic sentence. It should tell the main idea of your response. Use transition words like *then* and *however* to help your writing flow better.

Coached Reading

DIRECTIONS
Read the passage below. While you are reading, look to the Reading Guide for tips.

Faithfully Yours

Reading **Guide**

1   The kingdom was buzzing with excitement. The young queen had finally chosen her groom, the future king. Omar, the chosen groom, was envied by every other man in the land. Even his friends were filled with jealousy and spite.

2   As was the custom of this land, the queen departed on an adventure before they wed. She wrote her promised groom every day. The letters were tender and loving. Omar cherished every one. The queen ended each letter with the promise "Faithfully Yours."

> Notice how Omar feels about the letters that the queen sends at the beginning of her journey.

3   But then, one day, the letters stopped coming. Days passed, then weeks, and then months. No word was heard from the brave ruler. Years went by, but still Omar waited calmly for his royal bride to return. The men who once envied Omar now tormented him.

4   "You are a fool for waiting for your queen," they said with cruel smiles. "She will never come back for you."

5   Omar was hurt by the terrible words. His eyes stung with angry tears. But whenever his patience or hope began to fail, he looked back at her loving letters. "Faithfully yours," he would murmur, and he would feel at peace again.

> How does Omar comfort himself when his feelings begin to change?

6   One beautiful spring day, the queen finally returned. It had been a hard and dangerous journey. She was overjoyed to find her promised groom still waiting for her. "My beloved Omar," the queen exclaimed, "However did you wait for me so long?"

7   "My queen, I had your letters and I never lost faith in you."

> Omar reveals how he remained patient, calm, and faithful during the queen's long journey.

Independent Practice

DIRECTIONS

Use the passage to answer the extended-response question. As you write, pay close attention to the organization of your response. You may continue your answer on a separate sheet of paper if you run out of room below.

Omar's feelings do not change much during the queen's journey. How does he feel at the beginning of her journey? How does he feel at the end of her journey? What causes his feelings to remain mostly the same? Use details from the story to support your answer.

In your answer, be sure to include

- how Omar feels at the beginning of the queen's journey
- how Omar feels at the end of the queen's journey
- what causes Omar's feeling to remain mostly the same
- details from the story to support your answer

_____

_____

_____

_____

_____

_____

_____

_____

27 Language

Getting the Idea

A good writer chooses his or her words carefully. The right **word choice** can help the reader understand and enjoy the writing.

When writing, use a variety of words. Try to use words that mean exactly what you want to say. Descriptive words can help a reader picture what the writer is imagining. Read these two examples. Which one is stronger?

- Clouds moved across the sky.
- Dark rain clouds raced over the gloomy sky.

You should also use different kinds of sentences in writing. This is called **sentence variety**. Sentences do not all have to begin the same way. Sentences also do not have to be the same length. It is good to write some long sentences and some short sentences. This makes the writing seem smoother and gives it rhythm.

Suppose you want to describe a football game. You can begin a sentence about it in different ways to make it more interesting.

- Basic thought: The crowd watched the football game.
- Add a descriptive word or words: The excited crowd watched the football game.
- Add a phrase: Cheering loudly, the crowd watched the football game.

A writer's **voice** is how his or her writing sounds to the reader. Each writer has a different voice. A writer's voice shows his or her personality.

A writer's voice should be right for the topic. For example, when writing an e-mail to a friend, a writer uses a friendly voice. It sounds like the writer is talking to a friend. But what if a writer is writing a letter to a newspaper editor? In that case, the writer should use a different, more formal voice.

Coached Example

DIRECTIONS
Read this passage and answer the question that follows. Write your answer on a separate sheet of paper.

Alicia stood beside the swollen river with her mother. The trip had taken much longer than usual. The wind had kept pushing them back like an invisible hand.

Alicia could see that the raging river was rising. It was a monster that had torn away the bridge. How would they get to town to meet Papa's train? How would he get home to them? Alicia grasped her mother's hand. It was cold but damp with sweat.

The pair had been silent during most of the walk. The wind would have swallowed their words anyway. Now that Alicia was standing still, the cold snatched away all the warmth from her body. She wanted to comfort her mother, but she was tongue-tied. All she could do was clutch her mother's hand tighter.

Thinking It Through

Think about how you feel while reading this passage. What words does the author use to make you feel this way? Use details from the story to support your answer.

In your answer, be sure to include

- how the passage makes you feel
- what words the author uses to create this feeling
- details from the story to support your answer

HINT Think about who will be reading your response. Should you write this response like a formal report, or like a letter to your best friend? Remember to use descriptive details to support your answer. You should also vary your sentences to make your response more interesting.

Lesson Practice

Coached Reading

DIRECTIONS
Read the passage below. While you are reading, look to the Reading Guide for tips.

Voyage Across the Pacific

1   Thor Heyerdahl was a brave explorer from Norway. One of the most exciting adventures he set out on was a voyage by raft from Peru to the Polynesian Islands. He and his crew had to sail over 4,000 miles on the Pacific Ocean to make this journey.

2   At first, the dark rough seas hid whatever life swam beneath the small wooden raft. Then the churning ocean grew calm and as smooth as glass. A rich world filled with life was revealed in the crystal-clear water.

3   An eight-foot-long shark was one of the raft's first visitors. The grayish-blue shark rolled over and showed its enormous white belly. Throughout the voyage, huge sharks stalked nearby. They had razor-sharp teeth and eyes like a cat's. Whenever the crew saw a menacing fin, they would not swim in the ocean.

4   Harmless foot-long pilot fish swam around the fierce sharks. These pale-blue fish had dark stripes that ran from their faces to their tails. To the delight of the crew, some of the pilot fish abandoned their sharks and stayed with the raft.

5   The crew also became friendly with tiny crabs. They were the size of a fingernail and moved very fast. They named one of them "Johannes" and kept it as a pet.

6   The most meaningful animal to Thor and his crew was the frigate bird. This bird species has mostly black feathers, with white feathers on its belly. When Thor saw a flock flying overhead, he knew they were near land and that the long voyage was over!

Reading Guide

These paragraphs describe the explorers, their voyage, and the ocean. However, no other living things are mentioned.

The crew thinks of the sharks' fins as menacing. The men do not go into the water when they see them. What does this reveal about their thoughts toward sharks?

Notice words that describe the color and size of the various living things.

Independent Practice

DIRECTIONS
Use the passage to answer the extended-response question. As you write, pay close attention to your word choice and voice. You may continue your answer on a separate sheet of paper if you run out of room below.

In the passage "Voyage Across the Pacific," Thor and his crew encounter many different forms of life at sea. Describe each living thing they saw. How does information from "Voyage Across the Pacific" show what Thor and his crew felt about each of these living things? Use details from the passage to support your answer.

In your answer, be sure to include

• what forms of life Thor and his crew saw at sea
• a description of each living thing
• how Thor and his crew felt about each living thing
• details from the passage to support your answer

_____

_____

_____

_____

_____

_____

_____

Directions
Read this article. Then answer question 1.

Amelia Earhart

by Charlotte Petrova

In the 1920s and 1930s, many women in the United States did not work outside the home—they were homemakers. The women who did work outside the home were usually teachers, nurses, or office workers. However, some women wanted other jobs that were mostly held by men. These women had big dreams. They wanted to make them come true. One of these women was named Amelia Earhart.

As a young woman, Amelia worked as a nurse. She helped people in a military hospital. Then she went to school to study medicine. She visited her family in California. They went to an air show. She was interested in the airplanes. The next day, she went for a short plane flight. She was hooked. Amelia decided that she wanted to be a pilot.

Amelia stopped studying medicine. She started learning how to fly. Her teacher was a female pilot named Anita Snook. After learning to fly, Amelia traveled for a while. She made news in different cities. Most people had never heard of a woman who could fly a plane!

In 1927, Charles Lindbergh flew across the Atlantic Ocean. He was the first person to do it by himself. A year later, Amelia was the first woman to fly across the Atlantic. Two men named Wilmer Stultz and Slim Gordon were actually the pilots. Amelia was only a passenger. But, the newspapers did not care. They said Amelia was the first woman to make the trip. They called her "Lady Lindy," after Charles Lindbergh. This upset her, because she did not really fly the plane. She decided to set this right. In 1932, Amelia did become the first woman to fly across the Atlantic alone.

Amelia was very successful as a pilot. But she had one more goal. She wanted to be the first woman to fly around the world. In 1937, Amelia took off from Oakland, California. She had a copilot with her. They flew to Florida and Puerto Rico. Then they went to South America and Africa. Finally, they flew on to Asia.

After that, their plane disappeared. They were flying from Asia to Australia. Nobody knows what happened to them.

We may never know what became of Amelia. However, she will always be admired. She was a daring woman and a fearless pilot.

You may plan your writing on a separate sheet of paper.

1

Think about Amelia Earhart from the article and other American women of the 1920s and 1930s. How were they **alike**? What did they do that was the same? How were they **different**? How was what they did different? Use details from the article to support your answer.

In your answer, be sure to

- tell how Amelia and other American women were alike
- explain how what they did was the **same**
- tell how Amelia and other American women were different
- explain how what they did was **different**
- use details from the article to support your answer

_____

_____

_____

_____

_____

_____

Go On

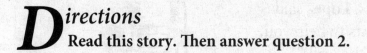

Directions
Read this story. Then answer question 2.

The School Mural

by Dave Kowalski

Wylie Jacobs walked to his elementary school to practice tennis every Saturday morning. He went to a wall on the south side of the school. It was perfect for practicing his shots. The wall had a smooth surface. Beneath the dust and graffiti, Wylie could still see the faint outline of an old painting on the wall. He sometimes tried to figure out what the painting had been. It was hard to tell since it had become so faded.

One morning, Wylie was surprised to see a group of people measuring the wall. "Sorry," a young woman in overalls said. "You can't play here. We're going to cover the wall with bricks. It's in bad shape and we want to make it look new."

"I guess I'll have to find a new place to practice my tennis," Wylie said to his dad when he came back home. "There were some workers at the school this morning. They were getting ready to cover the old wall with bricks."

His dad was quiet. Then he asked, "Is that mural of the school still there?"

"Mural of the school?" Wylie asked. "You mean that old painting on the wall?"

"When we painted it, we thought it would last," said Wylie's dad, with a sigh. "I guess we were wrong."

"You painted it?" Wylie asked.

"The rest of the students and I did," his dad said.

Wylie imagined the hard work that went into the mural. He came up with an idea. On Monday, Wylie arrived at school early. He knocked on the principal's door.

"Hi, Wylie," Ms. Lopez said. "How can I help you?"

"I want to repaint the mural that is on the wall on the south side of the building," Wylie pleaded.

Go On

"A mural is a BIG project." Ms. Lopez said. "If you can get some other students to help you, then I'll cancel the plans to brick the wall."

Wylie jumped out of his seat. "Thank you, Ms. Lopez!" he said, smiling.

The next day, Wylie told all the grades about his plan. By the end of the day, more than thirty students had signed up to help.

"Ms. Lopez," he said running into her office. "Over thirty students have signed up. Can we do it?"

"You can start next week," she smiled. "I'll call the company to have them clean the wall instead of laying bricks over it."

By the next week, the workers had put a coat of white paint on the wall. The day after that, Wylie's dad helped him plan the new mural on paper. Then he and his dad used black paint to outline the mural on the wall.

"I remember doing this thirty years ago," Wylie's dad said. "I can't wait to see the finished project."

For the next few weeks, many students came to help. They painted the colors and details in the mural. For each part, they would look at Wylie's plan to see which colors to use. The team went through gallons of paint to cover the wall. Each day, more and more students showed up. Some of their parents even started coming to help out.

A few weeks later, Wylie was amazed. Now there was a beautiful mural brightening up the whole side of the school.

Ms. Lopez threw a school party to celebrate. All of the kids and their parents were invited. Wylie went with his dad. His dad couldn't take his eyes off of the painted wall.

"This is even better than it was when I painted it," his dad said, putting his hand on Wylie's shoulder.

Ms. Lopez stood in front of the mural to speak. "I am very proud of all the students who worked so hard to paint the new mural," she said. "Especially Wylie Jacobs!"

You may plan your writing on a separate sheet of paper.

2

Wylie's dad's feelings change in the story. How does he feel at the beginning of the story? How does he feel at the end of the story? What causes his feelings to change? Use details from the story to support your answer.

In your answer, be sure to include

- how Wylie's dad feels at the beginning of the story
- how Wylie's dad feels at the end of the story
- what causes Wylie's dad's feelings to change
- details from the story to support your answer

_____

_____

_____

_____

_____

_____

_____

_____

_____

Go On

STOP

CHAPTER

6 Writing Mechanics

28 Punctuation

Getting the Idea

Punctuation is the group of marks that are used in sentences. Some punctuation marks are found at the end of sentences. These are periods (.), question marks (?), and exclamation marks (!).

Examples: I went to the store.

Did you talk to your teacher?

Look at that bear!

Commas (,) separate items in a list. They also separate parts of addresses.

Examples: I bought milk, bread, eggs, and butter at the store.

The main store is in Chicago, Illinois.

Quotation marks (" ") show what someone says or has said. Place quotation marks around what is said. Include any other punctuation inside the quotation marks. You may need to use a comma to separate the rest of the sentence from what is said.

Examples: "Did you want lunch?" Chris asked.

Ravenna said, "No, thank you. I just ate."

You may also use quotation marks with titles of stories, poems, and articles.

Apostrophes show ownership when used with a noun.

Examples: Maya's book   Ryder's pencil

Apostrophes are also used with contractions. A **contraction** is a shortened form of a word or words. The apostrophe shows missing letters.

Words	Contraction	Words	Contraction
I am	I'm	we are	we're
he has	he's	we have	we've
it has	it's	you have	you've

Coached Example

DIRECTIONS
Read this passage and answer the questions that follow.

When Amina saw her friend Nolan, she said, "Hi, Nolan! What did you do yesterday?"

Nolan said, "I went to the zoo with my family."

What kind of animals did you see? Amina asked.

"I saw all kinds of strange animals," he replied. "But since their names are so hard to say, I have to write them down."

Here is the list of strange animals that Nolan showed to Amina:

a giraffe
a flying fox
a toucan
a blue morpho

 **Thinking It Through**

1. How could you write Nolan's list as a series with commas?

    A. giraffe flying fox toucan blue morpho

    B. a giraffe a flying fox, a toucan, a blue morpho

    C. a giraffe, a flying fox a toucan, a blue morpho

    D. a giraffe, a flying fox, a toucan, a blue morpho

    HINT A comma goes after each item in a series *except* the last item.

2. Which sentence is punctuated correctly?

    A. "What kind of animals did you see? Amina asked.

    B. "What kind of animals did you see"? Amina asked.

    C. "What kind of animals did you see?" Amina asked.

    D. "What kind of animals did you see" Amina asked.

    HINT Think about when and how to use quotation marks and end marks.

Lesson Practice

Coached Reading

DIRECTIONS
Read the passage below. While you are reading, look to the Reading Guide for tips.

Excerpted from

Freedom

by Francis C. Woodworth

Reading Guide

1   Soon after the war ended, a boy was selling some caged birds in a town. He had a blue bird, a red bird, a yellow bird, and a green bird. A sailor came up and asked how much they were.

How is the list of birds punctuated?

2   "Five dollars each," said the boy.

3   I did not ask the price of each, said the sailor. "How much for all of them?"

In paragraph 2, why is the boy's reply to the sailor in quotation marks?

4   The boy thought for a moment. Then he answered. "Fifteen dollars," he said.

5   The sailor handed him the money. The sailor then opened the cage door and let the birds go free.

6   The surprised boy cried out, "What are you doing? You'll lose your birds!"

7   "Thats fine" said the sailor. "I've been locked up for three years as a prisoner of war. I decided never to keep anything in prison that I can make free."

What different end marks do you see in this passage?

Independent Practice

DIRECTIONS
Use the passage to answer questions 1–4.

1. Which sentence has a series with commas in it?

   A. Soon after the war ended, a boy was selling some caged birds in a town.

   B. He had a blue bird, a red bird, a yellow bird, and a green bird.

   C. "Five dollars each," said the boy.

   D. "I did not ask the price of each," said the sailor.

2. Which sentence correctly uses quotation marks?

   A. I did not ask the price of each, said the sailor.

   B. "I did not ask the price of each, said the sailor."

   C. "I did not ask the price of each," said the sailor.

   D. "I did not ask the price of each, said" the sailor.

3. Which sentence is punctuated correctly?

   A. "That's fine" said the sailor.

   B. "Thats fine," said the sailor.

   C. "That's fine." said the sailor.

   D. "That's fine," said the sailor.

4. In paragraph 6, what does the contraction *You'll* stand for?

   A. you will

   B. you are

   C. you do

   D. you have

29 Capitalization

Getting the Idea

Capitalization means using capital, or uppercase, letters. There are several rules about capitalization:

1. The first word of every sentence begins with a capital letter.

   Examples:

   We shook hands.

   The dog ran across the field.

2. The first word in direct quotations begins with a capital letter.

   Examples:

   Kyla asked, "May I borrow a pencil?"

   "Please sit down," the teacher said.

3. The first letter of a proper noun is capitalized. A **proper noun** is a name of a certain person, place, or thing.

   Examples:

   Abraham Lincoln   Mary Richardson Jones

   Jenny   Aunt Oma

   Chicago   Illinois

4. The first letter of certain adjectives is capitalized. These adjectives refer to specific places or cultures.

   Examples:

   the American flag   a French city

   a Native American drum   the Spanish language

Coached Example

DIRECTIONS
Read this passage and answer the questions that follow.

Mike ran into the garage to get his bicycle. He was excited to ride into town for the grand opening of Kiddie toyland. His friend, Luis, had come over so they could ride their bikes there together.

Luis asked, "what do you think they will have there?"

"I hope they have action figures and puzzles," said Mike. "My mom gave me money, and she said I have to buy either an action figure or a puzzle with it."

 **Thinking It Through**

1. Which is the correct capitalization for the name of the toy store?

   A. Kiddie toyland

   B. kiddie toyland

   C. Kiddie Toyland

   D. kiddie Toyland

   HINT Capitalize proper nouns, such as the names of places.

2. Which sentence has correct capitalization?

   A. Luis asked, "what do you think they will have there?"

   B. Luis asked, "What do you think they will have there?"

   C. luis asked, "What do you think they will have there?"

   D. luis asked, "what do you think they will have there?"

   HINT Find the quotation in the passage. Then review the rules of capitalization.

DIRECTIONS
Read the passage below. While you are reading, look to the
Reading Guide for tips.

Harriet Tubman and the Underground Railroad

Reading Guide

1   Harriet Tubman was a woman who had once been
a slave. She started life as Harriet Ross. She was born
in Dorchester County, maryland. In those days, close
records were not kept when slaves were born. So the
exact year of her birth is not known. However, she is
believed to have been born in either 1819 or 1820.

What is the rule for capitalizing place names, such as states?

2   Harriet had a difficult life growing up. When she was
25, she married a man named John Tubman. He was a
free african american. Harriet soon feared she would be
sold as a slave and forced to move to the South. With
the help of a white neighbor, she was able to escape
to Pennsylvania. It was there that she met people who
taught her about the Underground Railroad.

Why is *John Tubman* capitalized?

3   The Underground Railroad was not a real railroad.
It was a secret group of people with a plan to help slaves
escape to freedom. Harriet became involved.

4   The Underground Railroad was an organized system,
but it was still very dangerous. People who were slaves
were helped to get away from their slaveholders at night.
They traveled 10 to 20 miles to the next safe place.
There, someone would feed them and allow them to rest
before the next part of their journey.

5   The people were brought to northern states or to
canada. Because of the work of the Underground
Railroad, about 100,000 people escaped slavery.

Independent Practice

DIRECTIONS
Use the passage to answer questions 1–4.

1. What is the correct capitalization of the following place?

   A. Dorchester County, maryland

   B. Dorchester County, Maryland

   C. dorchester county, Maryland

   D. Dorchester county, Maryland

2. Why is *Underground Railroad* capitalized?

   A. It is part of a list.

   B. It is the beginning of a quotation.

   C. It is used as a proper name.

   D. It starts a sentence.

3. Which sentence has correct capitalization?

   A. The people were brought to northern states or to canada.

   B. The people were brought to Northern States or to Canada.

   C. The people were brought to Northern States or to canada.

   D. The people were brought to northern states or to Canada.

4. Which of the following uses correct capitalization?

   A. african american

   B. African American

   C. african American

   D. African american

30 Spelling

Getting the Idea

When spelling, there are some rules to remember.

A **compound word** is a word made of two smaller words.

> Example: snow + man = snowman

Homophones are words that are pronounced the same, but have different spellings and meanings.

> Example: *Plain* means "ordinary." *Plane* means "an airplane."

There are other spelling rules, too. Any word in the English language that has a *q* must have a *u* follow it.

> Examples: *quick*, *quack*, and *quiet*

Sometimes the spelling of a root word must be changed to add a suffix, such as *-ing* or *-er*. In some cases, you must double a consonant before adding the suffix. In other cases, you must change a *-y* at the end of a word to an *-i*. Study these examples.

Root Word	Add Suffix	Spelling Rule	New Word
bat	*-ing*	Double the consonant.	batting
happy	*-er*	Change the *-y* to *-i*.	happier

Some verbs seem to follow no rules when they are in different tenses.

Present	Past
hold	held
know	knew
feel	felt

When you are not sure how to spell a word, use a dictionary for help. In a dictionary, look for the first letter first, then the second, then the third.

Coached Example

DIRECTIONS

Read this passage and answer the questions that follow.

Ben's teacher taught his class how to alphabetize today. "You know the alphabet," Mr. Morris said. "Now you can use it in another way. Here is a list of words. First, put them in order by their first letter. Then, put them in order to the second letter. Then, try the third."

He listed the words on the board. Ben put them in order to the first letter:

apple, again, addition, dog, deck, drop, street, sack, state, zoo, zebra

"OK, now try to put the words in order to the second letter," said Mr. Morris.

Ben thought just about the words that started with the letter *a*. He put them in order:

addition, again, apple

"Good job!" said Mr. Morris. "Now try the rest."

Thinking It Through

1. Which word in the list comes after *deck* in alphabetical order?

   A. drop

   B. dog

   C. street

   D. sack

   HINT Put all the words that start with *d* in order by their second letter.

2. Which word in the list comes after *state* in alphabetical order?

   A. street

   B. sack

   C. zebra

   D. zoo

   HINT Put all the words that start with *s* in order by their second letters, and then by their third letters.

Lesson Practice

Coached Reading

DIRECTIONS
Read the passage below. While you are reading, look to the Reading Guide for tips.

The Spelling Bee

<table>
<tr><td>1</td><td>Julia looked through the list of words that might appear on the spelling bee. She went over them with her mom. The words were also on her vocabulary list, so she had to know their meanings.</td></tr>
<tr><td>2</td><td>"Test me now," said Julia. "Just tell me if I'm right or wrong."</td></tr>
<tr><td>3</td><td>Her mom asked her to spell the word that means the past tense of the word know.</td></tr>
<tr><td>4</td><td>"N-E-W," said Julia.</td></tr>
<tr><td>5</td><td>"No, that's wrong," said her mom. Next, she asked Julia to spell the past tense of the word worry.</td></tr>
<tr><td>6</td><td>"W-O-R-R-Y-E-D," replied Julia.</td></tr>
<tr><td>7</td><td>"No," said her mom. "But don't worry, you have time to practice. Do you think you can spell the word that means 'a big shake in the ground'?"</td></tr>
<tr><td>8</td><td>"E-A-R-T-H-Q-A-K-E?" asked Julia.</td></tr>
<tr><td>9</td><td>But she was wrong again. Her mom asked, "How about a word that means to pull something along the ground? But add an -ing suffix to the end of the word."</td></tr>
<tr><td>10</td><td>"All right, I think I can do that one. I think it's D-R-A-G-G-I-N-G, right?"</td></tr>
<tr><td>11</td><td>"Right!" her mother smiled.</td></tr>
</table>

Reading Guide

What kind of words are *knew* and *new*?

What is the rule about spelling a word with the letter *q*?

Independent Practice

DIRECTIONS
Use the passage to answer questions 1–4.

1. Which rule should Julia follow to spell the past tense of *worry*?

   A. the rule about doubling a consonant

   B. the rule about changing *-y* to *-i*

   C. the rule about making a compound word

   D. the rule about alphabetizing to the third letter

2. What is the correct spelling of the past tense of *know*?

   A. knowed

   B. new

   C. knew

   D. knowwing

3. What is the correct spelling of E-A-R-T-H-Q-A-K-E?

   A. earthquake

   B. earthqauke

   C. earthquacke

   D. earthquaky

4. Which rule did Julia follow to spell D-R-A-G-G-I-N-G correctly?

   A. the rule about using *qu*

   B. the rule about making a compound word

   C. the rule about changing *y* to *i*

   D. the rule about doubling a consonant

31 | Complete Sentences

Writing Mechanics Cluster

Getting the Idea

A **complete sentence** is a complete thought. A complete sentence starts with a capital letter and ends with a period, question mark, or exclamation mark. It must also have a subject and a verb.

Here are examples of complete sentences:

Lita loves the movies.

Does Hector want a sandwich?

I am so hungry!

When you are writing, be sure that each sentence is a complete thought. An incomplete sentence may look like a sentence but it is not. It has a capital letter at the beginning and a period at the end. But part of the sentence is missing. Read these examples:

Incomplete: Watching the movie. (THINK: *Who* is watching the movie?)

Complete: Tobin is watching the movie.

Incomplete: On the table. (THINK: *What* is on the table?)

Complete: The sandwich is on the table.

Also watch for **run-on sentences**. These are sentences that have two or more complete thoughts. They should be split apart into two sentences.

Incorrect: Remy is watching the soccer game he loves sports.

Correct: Remy is watching the soccer game. He loves sports.

Incorrect: Cho laughed at Emma's joke it was funny.

Correct: Cho laughed at Emma's joke. It was funny.

Coached Example

DIRECTIONS
Read this passage and answer the questions that follow.

Being with my stepfather is a special time. He works on projects in the garage. Sometimes he asks me to help out. Last week we hung a shelf on the wall I thought that was fun.

On Saturday after lunch, we went to the garage and started our project. First my stepfather cut the wood to the right size. Then he let me paint it. Finally, we put the shelf on the wall. I held the shelf while Dad screwed it in. When we were finished, he said the shelf was for me. Put my own tools on it.

Thinking It Through

1. Which sentence is a run-on sentence?

   A. Being with my stepfather is a special time.

   B. He works on projects in the garage.

   C. Sometimes he asks me to help out.

   D. Last week we hung a shelf on the wall I thought that was fun.

   HINT Think about which sentence has two complete thoughts.

2. Read this incomplete sentence.

   Put my own tools on it.

   How can you change it to make it a complete sentence?

   A. Am put my own tools on it.

   B. Put my own tools.

   C. I can put my own tools on it.

   D. My own tools on it.

   HINT Think about which choice has a subject and a verb.

Lesson Practice

Coached Reading

DIRECTIONS
Read the passage below. While you are reading, look to the Reading Guide for tips.

Sharks

Reading Guide

1   Sharks have changed very little in the last 150 million years. But why should they change? They are excellent at what they do.

2   Sharks are hunters that are very good at getting food. They use their keen sense of smell to find food. Their bodies can sense tiny vibrations in the water this helps them to locate their prey.

> Which sentence has two complete thoughts?

3   Sharks can grow new teeth. Unlike adult humans. When one tooth is lost or falls out, another will grow in its place. Sharks also have upper and lower jaws that both move. This makes a shark's jaws very powerful.

> Which sentence is NOT a complete thought?

4   Most sharks are meat eaters this means they hunt other animals for food. But some of the largest sharks are the least dangerous. Many of these larger sharks eat tiny sea plankton for food. They are not dangerous to larger fish or animals.

5   The most dangerous shark is the Great White Shark. This shark is responsible for more attacks on people than any other shark. While not the biggest shark. It is the largest of the fierce predator sharks.

6   Although people must be careful of sharks, they are also fascinated by them. Many people go to see sharks at aquariums across the country. There they learn about these amazing creatures.

Independent Practice

DIRECTIONS
Use the passage to answer questions 1–4.

1. What would be the BEST way to fix the run-on sentence from paragraph 2?

    A. Their bodies can sense. Tiny vibrations in the water this helps them to locate their prey.

    B. Their bodies can sense tiny vibrations in the water. This helps them to locate their prey.

    C. Their bodies can sense tiny vibrations. In the water this helps them to locate their prey.

    D. Their bodies can sense tiny vibrations in the water this helps them. To locate their prey.

2. Which would be the BEST way to fix the first two sentences of paragraph 3?

    A. Unlike adult humans, sharks can grow new teeth.

    B. Sharks can grow new teeth, however, unlike adult humans.

    C. Unlike adult humans. Sharks can grow new teeth.

    D. Sharks can grow new teeth but unlike adult humans.

3. Which of the following is an incomplete sentence?

    A. Many of these larger sharks eat tiny sea plankton for food.

    B. The most dangerous shark is the Great White Shark.

    C. While not the biggest shark.

    D. Sharks can grow new teeth.

4. Which sentence is a run-on sentence?

    A. They are not dangerous to larger fish or animals.

    B. Sharks also have upper and lower jaws that both move.

    C. Although people must be careful of sharks, they are also fascinated by them.

    D. Most sharks are meat eaters this means they hunt other animals for food.

32 Subject-Verb Agreement

Writing Mechanics Cluster

Getting the Idea

A **subject** is a person or thing that does the action in a sentence. A **predicate** contains a verb and tells the action of the subject. **Subject-verb agreement** is when the number of the subject matches the verb.

A simple subject is singular. The verb in the predicate must be singular.

> Example:
>
> *The book* <u>is on the shelf</u>.

A compound subject is plural. The verb in the predicate must be plural.

> Example:
>
> *Liza and Nicholas* <u>are at school</u>.

A compound predicate describes two actions.

> Example:
>
> *José* <u>plays baseball and writes stories.</u>

Sometimes a sentence is in the past tense. When this happens, the verb must be in the past tense.

> Example:
>
> *She* <u>curled</u> the ribbon.

Sometimes a phrase comes between the subject and the verb.

> Example:
>
> The *lady* who has three cats <u>was</u> at the store today.

Sometimes a singular subject can look like it is plural.

> Example:
>
> *One* of the boys in the class <u>is</u> sick.

Coached Example

DIRECTIONS
Read this passage and answer the questions that follow.

Dear Mrs. Garcia,

Please excuse Sandy from school on Monday. She had a difficult night on Sunday. When we returned home Sunday night from a weekend trip, we learned that our basement had flooded with water. My husband called a plumber, and the problem was fixed. However, Sandy and her brother were up late that night.

They finally fell asleep, but then they had trouble waking up in the morning. I did not want the children to go to school without proper rest.

I know Sandy had a math test on Monday. Please excuse her from the test and allow her to take it another time. I will allow her to stay after school any day you would like.

Thank you,

Mrs. Rahman

Thinking It Through

1. What is the subject of the sentence, "She had a difficult night on Sunday"?

   A. She

   B. had

   C. night

   D. Sunday

   HINT Think about who or what is the main focus of the sentence.

2. What is the verb in the sentence, "However, Sandy and her brother were up late that night"?

   A. Sandy

   B. Sandy and her brother

   C. were

   D. that

   HINT The verb is the action that describes what the subject does.

Lesson Practice

Coached Reading

DIRECTIONS
Read the passage below. While you are reading, look to the Reading Guide for tips.

A Million Questions

Reading Guide

1   Jake and Aubrey sat in the back seat of the car. "When will we get there?" Jake asked.

What is the subject and verb in the first sentence?

2   "We will not be there for another hour," his dad replied.

3   "Can we stop and get something to eat? I'm hungry," said Aubrey.

4   "We just stopped for lunch an hour ago," said their mom. "You can't be hungry again."

5   The children had never been on such a long car trip before. They was taking a family vacation to an amusement park. It was five hours away from their home.

What is the correct way to write, "They was taking a family vacation to an amusement park"? Why?

6   "He have a card game," said Aubrey.

7   "He *has* a card game," corrected Jake. "*I* have the game. I'm only one person, and it's my game. If the game belonged to both of us, I would say, '*We have* a card game.'"

8   "Be nice to your sister," said their mom. "She is just learning. You're doing very well, Aubrey."

9   "I know," said Aubrey. "I thinks I'm doing great."

10   "I *think* I'm doing great," corrected her mom. "Now why don't you play that card game?"

11   "There's no room back here to play a card game," said Jake. "Let's play a guessing game."

12   "OK," said Aubrey.

13   "Guess what animal I am. '*Baa, baaaaaa,*'" he said.

14   "I know!" said Aubrey. "Jake are a sheep!"

15   "Oh, boy," said Jake. "Dad, are we almost there?"

Independent Practice

DIRECTIONS
Use the passage to answer questions 1–4.

1. Read the following sentence.

   "He have a card game," said Aubrey.

   What is wrong with the sentence?

   A. The subject is plural and the verb is singular.

   B. The subject is singular and the verb is plural.

   C. There is no verb in the sentence.

   D. There is no subject in the sentence.

2. Read this sentence from the passage.

   "She is just learning."

   Which of the following shows how this sentence could be made plural?

   A. "They is just learning."

   B. "They just learning."

   C. "Are just learning."

   D. "They are just learning."

3. Read this sentence.

   "I thinks I'm doing great."

   How should this sentence be corrected?

   A. Change *I* to *They*.

   B. Change *I* to *We*.

   C. Change *thinks* to *think*.

   D. Change *thinks* to *thinking*.

4. Which version of Aubrey's last sentence uses correct subject-verb agreement?

   A. "Jake is a sheep!"

   B. "Jake not a sheep!"

   C. "Jake and Aubrey is a sheep!"

   D. "Jake are a sheep!"

6 Review

Directions
Read this article. Then answer questions 1 through 6.

Dr. Martin Luther King Jr.

(1) Dr. Martin Luther King Jr., was born on January 15, 1929, in Georgia. (2) Dr King worked for the rights of African american people in the United states. (3) During the 1950s, there were many laws that kept African Americans from having the same rights as white Americans. (4) Dr. King helped change these laws.

(5) Many of the speeches Dr. King gave is still famous today. (6) His most famous speech is called I Have a Dream. (7) In it, he tells of his dream that all people in the United States have equal rights and live together in peace.

(8) Dr. King did not believe that people should hurt others to get the things that were important to them. (9) He believed instead that people should talk peacefully about the issues and work to solve them without hurting others. (10) Dr. King and others worked hard to achieve his dream. (11) Today, all americans have the same rights.

(12) Although Dr. King worked for peace, some people did not agree with him. (13) Dr. King was killed on April 4, 1968, in Memphis, Tennessee. (14) We remember Dr. King by celebrating his birthday. (15) With a national holiday every January.

1 Which version of sentence 5 has correct subject-verb agreement?

   A Many of the speeches Dr. King gave is still famous today.
   B Many of the speeches Dr. King gave are still famous today.
   C Many of the speech Dr. King gave is still famous today.
   D Many of the speech Dr. King gave are still famous today.

2 Which version of sentence 6 has correct punctuation?

   A His most famous speech is called "I Have a Dream."
   B His most famous speech is called, I Have a Dream.
   C His most famous speech is called I Have a Dream.
   D His most famous speech is called, "I Have a Dream?"

3 Which word in sentence 11 should be capitalized?

   A all
   B americans
   C same
   D rights

4 Which sentence is incomplete?

   A sentence 3
   B sentence 4
   C sentence 10
   D sentence 15

Go On

5 Rewrite sentences 1 and 2 to show correct capitalization and punctuation.

_____

_____

_____

_____

_____

6 Rewrite sentences 14 and 15 to show correct sentence construction.

_____

_____

_____

_____

_____

Directions
Read this article. Then answer questions 7 through 13.

Soccer

(1) Soccer is a sport in which too teams compete against each other on a field. (2) The game date back more than two thousand years. (3) Probably started in China. (4) Today soccer is called "football" in all countrys except the United States. (5) In America, "football" is a different game with different rules.

(6) In the game of soccer, each team have 11 players. (7) Teams try to kick a ball into the other team's net. (8) When they do, it is called a goal. (9) Each team has a goalie, who tries to stop the ball from entering the net. (10) The goalie can use any part of his or her body to stop the ball.

(11) The other team members can use any part of their bodies to hit the ball, except for their hands or arms. (12) Players mainly use their feet to kick the ball they can also use their heads, knees, or even chests to move the ball.

(13) Soccer is probably the most popular sport in the world. (14) Every four years a Championship game called the world cup is played to decide the Best team in the world? (15) More people watch the world cup than the summer olympic's.

Go On

7 In sentence 1, which word is spelled incorrectly?

A sport

B too

C compete

D field

8 What is the correct spelling of "countrys"?

A countryes

B countrees

C countries

D countrys

9 Which version of sentence 6 shows correct subject-verb agreement?

A In the game of soccer, each team have 11 players.

B In the game of soccer, each team has 11 players.

C In the game of soccer, each teams have 11 players.

D In the game of soccer, each teams has 11 players.

10 Which of the following is a run-on sentence?

A sentence 7

B sentence 9

C sentence 10

D sentence 12

11 Rewrite sentences 2 and 3 to show correct sentence construction and subject-verb agreement.

_____

_____

_____

_____

_____

_____

12 Rewrite sentences 14 and 15 to show correct capitalization and punctuation.

_____

_____

_____

_____

_____

_____

Go On

*D*irections

Now you will answer an extended-response question. You may plan your writing on a blank sheet of paper. Write your final answer on the lines below. If you run out of space, you may finish writing your response on a separate sheet of paper.

13

This article describes the game of soccer and how it is played. It also discusses soccer's popularity throughout the world. Why did the author most likely write this article? How do you know? Use details from the article to support your answer.

In your answer, be sure to include

- what the author's purpose for writing the article is
- which traits of the article reveal its purpose
- details from the article to support your answer

Check your writing for correct spelling, grammar, capitalization, and punctuation.

_____

_____

_____

_____

_____

_____

STOP

Glossary

apostrophe (') a punctuation mark used in word to show missing letters in a contraction or to show ownership in a possessive (Lesson 28)

author's purpose an author's reason for writing, usually to entertain, inform, or persuade (Lesson 17)

capitalization the use of uppercase letters at the beginning of sentences, with proper nouns, and with the word I (Lesson 29)

caption words beneath a graphic that describe what the graphic shows (Lesson 8)

cause the reason that something happens (Lesson 3)

characters the people, animals, or objects a story is about (Lesson 13)

chart a graphic organizer that is broken up into columns and rows, with headings that tell you what information is in each column and row (Lesson 9)

comma (,) a punctuation mark used to separate items in a list or separate a group of words in a sentence (Lesson 28)

compare to show how two or more things are alike (Lesson 4)

complete sentence a sentence made up of one complete thought with both a subject and a predicate (Lesson 31)

compound word two or more words combined to make one bigger word (Lesson 30)

conclusion a decision readers make about an entire text based on details, inferences, and what they already know (Lesson 11)

conflict the main problem of the story (Lesson 14)

context clues the words or sentences around a new word that help the reader understand its meaning (Lesson 10)

contraction a word that is made up of two other words, using an apostrophe to replace missing letters (Lesson 28)

contrast to show how two or more things are different (Lesson 4)

detail a piece of information that tells about the main idea (Lessons 1, 2, and 25)

directions a list of steps the reader should follow in order to complete a task (Lesson 6)

effect what happens as a result of a cause (Lesson 3)

exaggeration a statement that stretches the truth in order to make a point (Lesson 20)

fact a statement that is always true and can be proved to be true (Lessons 18 and 20)

fiction a made-up story or idea (Lesson 18)

graphic organizer a visual representation that helps you picture, arrange, and think about information (Lessons 9 and 22)

graphics pictures, drawings, and other visuals that go along with a text (Lesson 8)

heading a short title that tells the reader what a section of text is about (Lesson 8)

homophones words that sound the same but have different meanings (Lesson 30)

index an alphabetical list of important topics from the book and the page where each topic appears. It is found at the back of the book (Lesson 7)

inference a guess a reader makes about a text, based on the text's details and what the reader already knows (Lesson 11)

key words main words about your topic that you can use to find information in a text (Lesson 8)

main idea what a passage is mostly about (Lessons 2 and 25)

opinion a personal belief that cannot be proven (Lesson 20)

organizational features the parts of a text that help readers better understand what they are reading and find information quickly (Lesson 7)

plot the events of a story (Lesson 14)

predicate the part of the sentence that tells what the subject is doing by using a verb (Lesson 32)

prediction a guess about what will happen later in a passage, based on what you already know and what you have read (Lesson 12)

proper noun the name of a specific person, place, or thing (Lesson 29)

punctuation marks used to make sentences clearer for the reader (Lesson 28)

quotation marks (" ") punctuation marks that show speech (Lesson 28)

resolution the part of the plot that shows how characters try to solve the conflict (Lesson 14)

run-on sentence two or more sentence parts combined without proper punctuation (Lesson 31)

sentence variety using sentences of different length that begin in different ways to make writing more interesting (Lesson 27)

sequence the order in which events happen (Lesson 14)

sequence chart a graphic organizer that shows how one event leads to another (Lesson 9)

setting the time and place a story happens (Lesson 15)

subheading a smaller heading title that tells the reader more detailed information about what a section of text is about (Lesson 8)

subject the person, place, or thing that performs the action in a sentence (Lesson 32)

subject-verb agreement the correct use of singular subjects with singular verbs, and plural subjects with plural verbs (Lesson 32)

summarize to retell the main idea and most important details of the passage (Lesson 5)

table of a contents a list of chapters and page numbers where each chapter begins, found in the front of a book (Lesson 7)

theme a story's message (Lessons 16 and 24)

title the name of the book or article (Lesson 7)

topic sentence a sentence that tells you the main idea of a paragraph, usually found at the beginning of the paragraph (Lesson 26)

trait a quality of a character that makes him or her unique (Lesson 13)

transition words words or phrases that link one idea to another, such as *however, next, finally, therefore,* and *on the other hand* (Lesson 26)

Venn diagram a graphic organizer that uses overlapping circles to compare and contrast two different things (Lesson 4)

voice how a passage sounds to a reader, based on the author's personal style of writing (Lesson 27)

web a kind of graphic organizer with a topic or main idea in the center and related information around it (Lesson 9)

word choice the words a writer uses to express ideas in a way the audience can understand (Lesson 27)

New York State, Empire Edition, English Language Arts, Grade 4

PRETEST
Book 1

Name: _____

TIPS FOR TAKING THE TEST

Here are some suggestions to help you do your best:

- Be sure to read carefully all the directions in the test book.
- Plan your time.
- Read each question carefully and think about the answer before choosing your response.

Reading

Directions
In this part of the test, you are going to do some reading. Then you will answer questions about what you have read.

Read this article. Then answer questions 1 through 7.

The Human Eye

by Joanna Fraioli

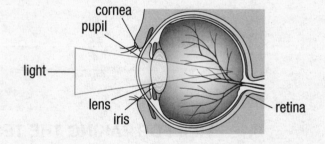

Vision, or how we see, is not a simple process. When we see, the eye gathers light that bounces off the things around us. The brain then changes that light into pictures or images. This forms what we "see."

The Path of Light

Light enters the eye through the cornea and the pupil and then passes through the lens. It passes through the inside of the eye until it hits the retina at the back of the eyeball. The light landing on the retina creates a small upside-down picture of the outside world. The retina is sensitive to light. Its job is to change the light into nerve impulses that are then sent to the brain. They are sent from the retina to the brain over the optic nerve.

The Amount of Light

We see best when there is just the right amount of light. Too little or too much light makes the picture unclear. The dark spot in the center of your eye is called the pupil. It controls the light entering the eye by changing size. When the light is dim, the pupil opens up wider to let as much light as possible into the eye. If the light is too bright, the pupil gets smaller and prevents too much light from getting in. And it does it all with help from your brain.

The Brain

The brain is where we really see the picture in a way that we understand it. Remember, the retina received and sent the picture upside down. So, the brain turns the picture the right side up again for us.

Both eyes send their own pictures. This means that the brain has to merge them into one. However, the brain also uses the two pictures for something very important. The pictures from the two eyes are never exactly the same. The differences between the pictures help the brain figure out how far away objects are from us.

Normal Vision

Eye doctors test your vision with a special eye chart. The chart has rows of letters. Each row of letters is smaller than the one above it. You read the rows of letters from a distance of 20 feet. You read the chart from top to bottom across each row until you can't see the letters clearly. Over the years, eye doctors have learned what a person should be able to see from 20 feet away. One row of letters is of this size. If you stand 20 feet away and can read this line, you have 20/20 vision. If you have 20/20 vision, your vision is normal.

1 According to the article, what happens if the pupil gets smaller?

A The picture becomes unclear.

B Less light is allowed into the eye.

C More light is allowed into the eye.

D The light does not land on the retina.

2 Read the sentence from the article.

This means that the brain has to merge them into one.

The word "merge" **most likely** means

A pull apart

B flip around

C make clearer

D bring together

Go On

3   What does the retina do while light is entering the eye?

   A It changes light into nerve impulses.

   B It connects the optic nerve to the brain.

   C It controls the amount of light that enters the eye.

   D It turns pictures of the outside world upside down.

4   Eye doctors ask people to read from a special eye chart from a distance of 20 feet because

   A that is how large most eye doctor's offices are

   B people cannot see anything from farther away than 20 feet

   C eye doctors think everyone has 20/20 vision

   D eye doctors know what normal vision is from that distance

5   Here is a web about the article.

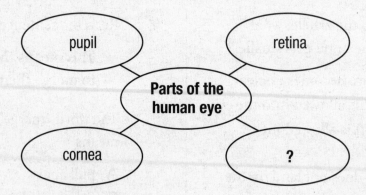

Which word could be added to this web?

A lens

B light

C brain

D eyeball

6 After reading the article, the reader could conclude that

    A vision is a simple process

    B light is not necessary for vision

    C the brain plays a key role in vision

    D people should visit the eye doctor often

7 The author **most likely** wrote this article in order to

    A teach readers how to see better

    B show readers how vision works

    C entertain readers with a story about eyes

    D persuade readers to buy glasses

Go On

The Canary

by Elizabeth Turner

Mary had a little bird,
With feathers bright and yellow,
Slender legs—upon my word,
he was a pretty fellow!

Sweetest notes he always sung,
Which much delighted Mary;
Often where his cage was hung,
She sat to hear Canary.

Crumbs of bread and dainty seeds
She carried to him daily,
Seeking for the early weeds,
She decked his palace gaily.

This, my little readers, learn,
And ever practice duly;
Songs and smiles of love return
To friends who love you truly.

Book 1

8   Which statement **best** describes the girl in the poem?

   A   The girl likes to sing.

   B   The girl enjoys decorating.

   C   The girl has no friends but the canary.

   D   The girl takes good care of her pet.

9   Why does Mary sit near Canary's cage?

   A   Canary wants something to eat.

   B   Mary wants to listen to the bird.

   C   Canary wants someone to play with.

   D   Mary wants to watch the pretty bird.

10   What does the poet compare to a palace?

   A   the bird's cage

   B   the early weeds

   C   the color of the bird

   D   the size of Mary's house

11   Which lines from the poem **best** tell the theme?

   A   "Slender legs—upon my word, / he was a pretty fellow!"

   B   "Often where his cage was hung, / She sat to hear Canary."

   C   "Seeking for the early weeds, / She decked his palace gaily."

   D   "Songs and smiles of love return / To friends who love you truly."

Go On

Pearly Whites

by Gavin McNulty

Amanda had a dentist appointment. She was not happy. She did not make the appointment, and she did not want to go. Her mother, however, insisted.

"It's been six months," Mom said. "You need to have a check-up."

"Come on, Mom," Amanda pleaded. "Can't I go next month? My teeth are fine."

Mom had made up her mind. She had scheduled the appointment for Friday.

On Thursday, Amanda stood in front of the bathroom mirror after brushing her teeth. She examined her teeth closely. Moments later, Amanda's older brother Paul saw her.

"What are you doing?" Paul asked.

"Nothing, Paul," Amanda replied. "Mind your business."

Paul smiled. He knew Amanda hated going to the dentist. He decided to have some fun with his sister.

"It's no surprise that Mom is making you go to the dentist," Paul began. "You haven't been there in so long."

"It's only been six months," Amanda said. "Plus, I brush twice a day."

"Six months is a long time," Paul continued. "Think of how much can happen in six months. You might need to have teeth pulled. The dentist may have to use one of his old, rusty drills on you. I'm sorry, Sis. You might be in trouble."

Amanda tried to ignore her brother. Unfortunately, while he talked, she thought she saw something. She noticed what looked like a tiny brown spot on one of her teeth. She hoped it was a shadow, but she was not sure. It could be a cavity.

Maybe Paul was right. Maybe the dentist would have to pull her teeth. Maybe he would use one of his old, rusty drills. Amanda's heart sank.

The next day, Amanda sat in the backseat of the car after school. Her appointment with Dr. Boucher was at 4:00. The clock in the car read 3:45.

Amanda's palms were sweaty. She could feel a lump in her throat. Her stomach did somersaults as Mom drove. She considered asking Mom once more to cancel the appointment but did not. Paul's warning from the day before rang in her ears.

"Hey, Mom," Amanda said. "How often does Dr. Boucher use his rusty drill?"

"What rusty drill?" Mom asked with a laugh. "Who put that idea in your head?"

Amanda's face became as red as a stoplight, and they drove on. They arrived at Dr. Boucher's office right on time. Amanda was in the dentist's chair at 4:01.

Dr. Boucher had gray hair and spoke softly. He asked Amanda about school and quickly set to work on her teeth. For twenty minutes, Amanda waited for him to open a drawer containing a pair of pliers and a rusty drill. She privately imagined how she would look with false teeth like Grandpa's.

Before Amanda knew it, Dr. Boucher was finished. He removed his rubber gloves and stood up. Amanda wiped her mouth and counted her teeth with her tongue. They were all there. Amanda breathed a sigh of relief. Dr. Boucher smiled broadly.

"Great work, Amanda," said Dr. Boucher to the young girl in his chair. "If only your brother took such good care of his teeth."

---

12 Read these sentences from the story.

> **On Thursday, Amanda stood in front of the bathroom mirror after brushing her teeth. She examined her teeth closely.**

Which word means about the same as "examined"?

A felt

B worried

C studied

D brushed

13 This passage is **most** like a

A fairy tale

B news story

C real-life story

D textbook article

Go On

14 Which event happens **first** in the story?

   A Mom drives Amanda to the dentist.

   B Paul decides to have fun with Amanda.

   C Amanda finds a brown spot on her tooth.

   D Amanda counts her teeth with her tongue.

15 Read the chart below.

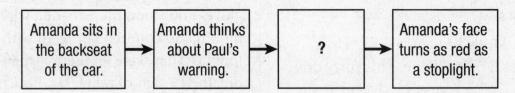

Which detail from the story **best** belongs in the empty box?

   A Amanda asks her mom about Dr. Boucher's rusty drill.

   B Amanda stands in front of the bathroom mirror.

   C Amanda and her mom arrive at Dr. Boucher's office on time.

   D Amanda thinks about asking her mom to cancel the appointment.

16 What will Amanda **most likely** do next?

   A check her teeth again

   B be afraid and start to cry

   C stop taking care of her teeth

   D go home and tease her brother

Directions
Read this article. Then answer questions 17 through 23.

A "Quick" Experiment

by Madeleine LaTour

A man is walking through a valley. Suddenly, he begins to sink into the earth. The more he moves, the faster he sinks. A soupy, thick mud is pulling him down. There is nothing he can do. He has been caught . . . in quicksand!

Recognize this scene? It's one that has appeared in countless action and adventure movies. The only thing is—that's not really how quicksand works. Quicksand is not as dangerous as you might think. Most quicksand is barely more than a few inches deep—and even if you were unlucky enough to fall into some really deep quicksand, you wouldn't sink any deeper than your waist. Actually, you'd begin to float. That's because people are lighter than quicksand.

How Quicksand Forms

Quicksand forms when water fills up an area of loose sand or soil. The water gets in between the grains of sand. It pushes them apart and causes them to lift up and tumble over one another. If the water cannot escape, the sand becomes liquefied. It is no longer solid enough to stand on.

Quicksand can form wherever there is water. It can form around lakes, ponds, rivers, marshes, and beaches. It can also form in an area that has an underground spring. For quicksand to form, there has to be a lot of moisture in the air, as well. Otherwise, the quicksand would evaporate.

DANGER: QUICKSAND

Go On

Book 1

Make Your Own Quicksand

Items Needed

- large mixing bowl
- newspaper
- 1 box of cornstarch (16 oz.)
- water

Directions

Step 1: Spread the newspaper out on top of a shelf or table in your kitchen. Place the large mixing bowl in the center of the newspaper.

Step 2: Add half of the box of cornstarch to the mixing bowl. Then very slowly add about one half-cup of water to the cornstarch, stirring the entire time. Keep adding the water and stirring the mixture until it gets about as thick as honey. Once it gets this thick, stop adding the water. This mixture will now be about as thick as quicksand.

Step 3: Stick your finger in the mixture. Move it slowly back and forth. Now try to move your finger quickly through the mix. Notice how hard it is to move your finger? It's almost impossible. The faster you move your finger, the thicker the mixture gets. The quick motion of your finger is causing the grains of cornstarch to clump together—just like the grains of sand in quicksand when we move quickly.

Step 4: Now move your finger slowly again. Notice how much easier it is to move? The grains of cornstarch have moved apart again and let the water back between them. The mixture is now more liquid than solid. This is just how quicksand works.

NOTE: When you are done, be sure to place your mixture in a plastic bag and throw it in the garbage. Pouring it down the drain will only cause it to thicken more and clog up your sink!

17 What should you do **right after** adding water to the cornstarch?

   A Add some more cornstarch.

   B Place newspaper under the bowl.

   C Move your finger in the cornstarch.

   D Stir the mixture of water and cornstarch.

18 According to the article, why does quicksand form?

   A Sand or soil becomes too loose.

   B Water gets in between grains of sand.

   C Air gets trapped in between grains of sand.

   D Grains of sand begin to multiply.

19 Based on the information in the section "Items Needed," which material will represent the sand in quicksand?

   A soil

   B water

   C cornstarch

   D newspaper

20 Which sentence from the article tells something that would **not** really happen?

   A "Suddenly, he begins to sink into the earth."

   B "If the water cannot escape, the sand becomes liquefied."

   C "Quicksand can form wherever there is water."

   D "Otherwise, the quicksand would evaporate."

Go On

21 According to the article, which statement about quicksand is **true**?

   A It can form anywhere and at anytime.

   B It thickens when things move quickly in it.

   C It forms when water falls on tightly packed sand.

   D It is extremely dangerous and cannot be avoided.

22 In which steps of "Make Your Own Quicksand" do you move your finger in the quicksand?

   A Steps 1 and 2

   B Steps 2 and 3

   C Steps 2 and 4

   D Steps 3 and 4

23 What information can be found in the section "How Quicksand Forms"?

   A an explanation of how to avoid quicksand

   B a description of how to make your own quicksand

   C a description of how quicksand develops in nature

   D an explanation of why quicksand in movies is not realistic

Directions

Read this story about a trip to the movie theater. Then answer questions 24 through 28.

Movie Night

by Aisha Carter

Malcolm hated to be late for movies. Unfortunately, the whole evening had been a series of delays. Now, Malcolm sat in the car. He was annoyed. The light was red. The car was stopped. He began to recall the events of the night.

At 6:00, Malcolm checked the movie times in the newspaper. He wanted to see *Jungle Cats*, but that was not playing nearby. *Sky Riders* did not end until after his bedtime. So, he would settle for *Stars and Stripes* or *The Good Detective*. *Stars and Stripes* started at 7:00. *The Good Detective* began at 7:30. Malcolm chose *The Good Detective*. He thought going to a later movie would give Ana more time.

Ana was Malcolm's sister. She was always late. For example, even though she knew that the movie began at 7:30, she did not get in the shower until 6:45. By the time Ana was dressed, it was 7:15. Ana left them less than fifteen minutes to drive to the theater. Malcolm's blood boiled thinking about it.

Then she had to put on make-up. Ana needed make-up because Darren, her new boyfriend, worked at the movie theater. Malcolm knew why Ana offered to take him to the movies. She wasn't just being kind. She just wanted to see Darren. He also knew that they were going to be late.

At 7:27, they were still in the car. The show would start in three minutes. Malcolm was not hopeful. It was Saturday night. The movie theater would be crowded. Viewers would be lined up to see the latest action movie or comedy. Malcolm looked at Ana. He wanted to tell her that they should just forget about the movies. At this rate, they would be lucky if they even found seats before the previews. It was Ana, however, who spoke. While Malcolm was nervous, Ana was calm.

"I know you cannot bear to be late," Ana said, "so I called Darren earlier. He's the one who turns on the projector for each show. He promised to save us seats that aren't too close to the screen. Also, he won't start the show until we get there."

Malcolm was speechless. He just smiled. Ana had really surprised him this time.

Go On

24 What is this story **mostly** about?

A a boy who dislikes his older sister

B a boy who wants to get to the movies on time

C a girl who is always late to things

D a girl who wants to meet her boyfriend at a movie theater

25 What is the **main** problem in the story?

A Ana is going to make Malcolm late to the movie.

B Malcolm cannot see *Jungle Cats* because it is not playing nearby.

C Ana is running so late that Malcolm misses a movie.

D Malcolm cannot see *Sky Riders* because it ends after his bedtime.

26 Why does Ana leave less than 15 minutes to drive to the theater?

A She cannot decide what movie to see.

B She does not realize the theater will be crowded.

C She showers late and puts on make-up for her boyfriend.

D She cannot decide which outfit she should wear.

27 Read the chart below.

Movie Time	Movie Title
7:00	?
7:30	*The Good Detective*

Which title **best** completes the chart?

A *Sky Riders*

B *Jungle Cats*

C *Movie Night*

D *Stars and Stripes*

28 Why did the author **most likely** write this story?

A to persuade readers to go to the movies

B to convince readers to act more responsibly

C to share ideas about how to solve a problem

D to entertain readers with a story about a brother and sister

STOP

New York State, Empire Edition,
English Language Arts, Grade 4

PRETEST
Book 2

Name: _____

TIPS FOR TAKING THE TEST

Here are some suggestions to help you do your best:

- Be sure to read carefully all the directions in the test book.
- Plan your time.
- Read each question carefully and think about the answer before choosing your response.

In this test, you will be writing about texts that you will be listening to or reading. Your writing will be scored on

- how clearly you organize your writing and express what you have learned
- how accurately and completely you answer the questions being asked
- how well you support your responses with examples of details from the text
- how correctly you use grammar, spelling, punctuation, capitalization, and paragraphing

Listening and Writing

D irections

In this part of the test, you are going to listen to a story called "Merlin and the Lady of the Lake." Then you will answer questions 29 through 31 about the story.

You will listen to the story twice. The first time you hear the story, listen carefully but do not take notes. As you listen to the story the second time, you may want to take notes. Use the space below and on the next page for your notes. You may use these notes to answer the questions that follow. Your notes on these pages will NOT count toward your final score.

Notes

Notes

Go On

29 The Lady of the Lake makes a plan to control Merlin's power. Complete the chart below to show how the plan is carried out.

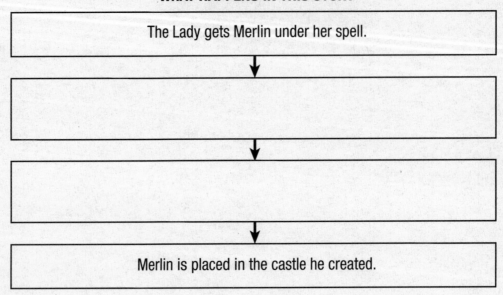

WHAT HAPPENS IN THIS STORY

The Lady gets Merlin under her spell.

↓

↓

↓

Merlin is placed in the castle he created.

30 Think about whether the Lady of the Lake and Merlin get what they want in the story. Now choose one of the characters:

Lady of the Lake   **Merlin**

Explain how the character you choose does or does not get what she or he wants. Use details from the story to support your answer.

_____

_____

_____

_____

_____

You may plan your writing for question 31 on a separate sheet of paper.

31

Think about Merlin and the Lady of the Lake from the story. How are they **alike**? How are they **different**? What happens to each of them because of their differences? Use details from the story to support your answer.

In your answer, be sure to

- tell how Merlin and the Lady of the Lake are **alike**
- tell how Merlin and the Lady of the Lake are **different**
- explain what happens to them because of their differences
- use details from the story to support your answer

Check your writing for correct spelling, grammar, capitalization, and punctuation.

_____

_____

_____

_____

_____

_____

_____

_____

_____

Go On

STOP

New York State, Empire Edition, English Language Arts, Grade 4

PRETEST

Book 3

Name: _____

TIPS FOR TAKING THE TEST

Here are some suggestions to help you do your best:

- Be sure to read carefully all the directions in the test book.
- Plan your time.
- Read each question carefully and think about the answer before writing your response.

In this test, you will be writing about texts that you will be listening to or reading. Your writing will be scored on

- how clearly you organize your writing and express what you have learned
- how accurately and completely you answer the questions being asked
- how well you support your responses with examples of details from the text
- how correctly you use grammar, spelling, punctuation, capitalization, and paragraphing

Book 3

Reading and Writing

Directions

In this part of the test, you are going to read a passage called "A Butterfly's Life" and a poem called "Born to Change." You will answer questions 32 through 35 and write about what you have read. You may look back at the passage and poem as often as you like.

A Butterfly's Life

by Pedro Ruiz

Have you ever spotted a colorful butterfly darting from one flower to another? Have you had one land on your hand or windowsill? Butterflies are quite wonderful. Long before they become creatures with wings, however, they are caterpillars.

Butterflies start out their lives as eggs. A mother butterfly usually lays 200 to 500 eggs at once! She lays her eggs on the leaves or stem of a plant. Different kinds of butterflies have different types of eggs. They come in many different shapes and sizes.

About five days after they are laid, the eggs begin to stir. When an egg hatches, it becomes a *larva*. Larva is another name for caterpillar. The caterpillars are very tiny when they hatch. They are also very hungry. They begin eating. First, they eat the eggshell they came out of. Then they start chewing on the closest leaf. It is not long until they have eaten enough that their skin no longer fits. It is far too small!

Slowly, the skin splits. The caterpillars wriggle free. They already have a new skin waiting underneath. They may be bigger, but they are still hungry. They start eating again. They chew through many leaves. It is not long before the new skin is too little again. Most caterpillars change their skin about five times.

After a few weeks, the caterpillars are finished eating and growing. When caterpillars are fully grown, they find a twig. They hang upside down from it. Once again, their skin splits. This time it covers them like a warm sleeping bag. The outside of the skin turns hard. This becomes the cocoon.

- - - - - - - - - - - - - - - - - - - -

Inside a cocoon, the larva becomes a *pupa*. A pupa is just a caterpillar inside its cocoon. But amazing things are happening inside those hard little shells. The pupas are resting and changing. For weeks, or sometimes months, the cocoon is quiet and still. Finally, one day it splits open. The caterpillar has transformed into a butterfly!

The butterfly's head and legs come out first. Butterflies do not look very pretty yet. Their wings are crumpled and flat. After a while, they are able to pump blood into their wings. They start to unfold. The bright colors are seen for the first time.

Butterflies cannot fly until their new wings dry and stiffen. They rest on a plant or a rock in the sun. They slowly move their wings. As soon as they are ready, the new creatures spread their wings. Each butterfly is now free to flutter in the breeze.

The butterflies begin searching for something to eat. Actually, butterflies cannot really eat—they drink all their food. Each butterfly has a long tube in its mouth. It uses its tube like we use a straw. The butterflies drink nectar from flowers, or juice from fruits. They may also take a tiny sip of water from a puddle.

Sadly, the butterfly does not have long to drink in life. Most butterflies only live for about two weeks. In that short time, the butterflies must find a mate. Then the female butterflies lay their own eggs. After that, the cycle of butterfly life can begin again.

Go On

32 What happens to the caterpillar after it is finished eating and growing? Use details from the passage to support your answer.

_____

_____

_____

_____

_____

_____

Book 3

Born to Change

by Carol Cassidy

Born hungry,
You eat your first home.
You keep munching
And changing your clothes
To make more room.

You grow and eat,
Eat and grow,
Until the time comes
When you stop getting bigger
And go upside down instead.

In an old pattern,
You split one more time,
Covering up in a blanket
And beginning to change
From long to lovely.

Time goes on—
A quiet time—
Until a special day
When you come out
As something new.

Wet and waiting
For flight to come,
You soar to the sky
To live a short life—
A matter of days.

Flying to backyards,
Visiting briefly
Pretty flowers,
And then laying eggs
To begin again.

Go On

33 At the end of the poem, why is there a new beginning when the creature lays eggs? Use details from both the poem and passage to support your answer.

_____

_____

_____

_____

_____

34 The poem describes the life cycle of a living creature. Each part of the poem tells a different part of the cycle. Complete the chart below to show what happens in each stanza. Two boxes have been completed for you.

Part	What Happens
1	The creature is born. It eats and begins to grow.
2	The creature keeps growing then turns upside down.
3	
4	
5	
6	

Go On

Book 3

Planning Page

You may PLAN your writing for question 35 here if you wish, but do NOT write your final answer on this page. Your writing on this Planning Page will not count toward your final score. Write your final answer on Pages 227 and 228.

35

The poem "Born to Change" describes the life of a living creature. Explain what this creature is and how it changes. How does information from "A Butterfly's Life" show that the poem is based on facts? Use details from **both** the passage and the poem to support your answer.

In your answer, be sure to include

- what creature is described in the poem
- how the creature changes
- how the passage shows that the poem is based on facts
- details from **both** the passage and the poem to support your answer

Check your writing for correct spelling, grammar, capitalization, and punctuation.

_____

_____

_____

_____

_____

_____

_____

_____

_____

_____

Go On

STOP

New York State, Empire Edition, English Language Arts, Grade 4

POSTTEST
Book 1

Name: _____

TIPS FOR TAKING THE TEST

Here are some suggestions to help you do your best:

- Be sure to read carefully all the directions in the test book.
- Plan your time.
- Read each question carefully and think about the answer before choosing your response.

Reading

Directions
In this part of the test, you are going to do some reading. Then you will answer questions about what you have read.

Read this story. Then answer questions 1 through 5.

The Riddle of the Sphinx

a story from ancient Greece

Outside the city of Thebes lived a horrible creature known as the Sphinx. She had the face of a woman, the claws and strength of a lion, the tail of a snake, and the wings of a bird. People were terrified of her, not so much because of her appearance, but rather because of her game.

Whenever someone wanted to go into or out of Thebes, they had to go quickly and quietly in the night while the Sphinx was sleeping. If they did not, they would be forced to play her game. The Sphinx's game consisted of a single riddle. If the person could answer the riddle, he or she would be allowed to pass. Those who could not give the correct answer, the Sphinx would kill!

For many years, no one could answer the riddle, so many people died. One day, a man named Oedipus wanted to go to Thebes. As he prepared to enter the city, the Sphinx swooped down from her perch and stood in front of him. Oedipus drew his sword, but she quickly snatched it from him and threw it away.

"What do you want of me, beast?" Oedipus asked.

"I ask only that which I ask all others," replied the Sphinx. "I ask that you solve my riddle. If you give the correct answer, you may pass. If you do not, I shall kill you!"

Oedipus knew that he would never be able to outrun the creature. He also knew that, without his rapier, he could not kill the monster either. "Fine," he said, "Tell me your riddle!"

The Sphinx replied, "What creature walks in the morning on four feet, at noon on two feet, and in the evening on three?"

"Hmmm… let me think," Oedipus replied, trying to think of all the animals he knew. "Dogs walk on four feet, unless they hurt a paw, then they limp. They never walk on two feet, though," he thought to himself.

"I do not have all day!" the Sphinx soon said, getting angry with Oedipus for not answering.

Try as he might, though, Oedipus could not think of any creature that walked like this. He thought to himself, "Why, the only animal I can think of that walks on two feet is… that's it!"

"The answer is a man!" he proclaimed. "When we are babies, in the morning of our lives, we crawl on all fours. When we grow to adulthood, at the noontime of our lives, we walk on two feet. When we grow old, in the evening of our lives, we use a cane, walking on three feet!"

He was right! The fabled riddle of the Sphinx had been solved! The Sphinx was so angry at Oedipus for ruining her game that she burst into flame, and was never seen nor heard from again. Oedipus made his way into Thebes.

1 Read these sentences from the story.

> **Oedipus knew that he would never be able to outrun the creature. He also knew that, without his rapier, he could not kill the monster either.**

Which word means about the same as "rapier"?

A army

B shield

C sword

D strength

2 Which event tells the reader that this story could **not** really have happened?

A A man tries to enter the city of Thebes.

B A difficult riddle is finally solved.

C People had to sneak out of Thebes at night.

D A creature called the Sphinx bursts into flames.

Go On

3 What will **most likely** happen next in the story?

   A The Sphinx will return and punish Oedipus.

   B Oedipus will turn around before getting to Thebes.

   C Oedipus will face another evil creature with a riddle.

   D The people of Thebes will celebrate Oedipus's victory.

4 Which word **best** describes Oedipus?

   A selfish

   B clever

   C kind

   D curious

5 Read the chart below.

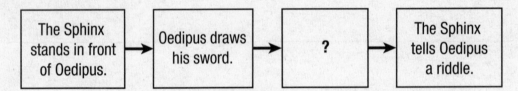

The Sphinx stands in front of Oedipus. → Oedipus draws his sword. → ? → The Sphinx tells Oedipus a riddle.

Which event **best** fits in the empty box?

   A Oedipus solves the riddle.

   B Oedipus makes his way to Thebes.

   C The Sphinx takes away the sword.

   D The Sphinx gets impatient and angry.

Directions
Read this article. Then answer questions 6 through 13.

We Can Do It!

by Elizabeth Serra

When the United States entered World War II, a lot of men joined the army. This meant that there were a lot of soldiers to fight for our freedom. It also meant that there were a lot of jobs that were not being done, because the men were off fighting.

What happens to an airplane factory when all of its workers leave? It stops making airplanes! We could not let this happen. Without planes and other supplies, we would lose the war. To keep the factories open, owners started to hire women.

At this time, most women were homemakers. If a woman had a job outside of the home, it was usually a job held mostly by women, such as nurse or teacher. A lot of people thought that women were not as good workers as men. These people were wrong.

The government created a poster to encourage women to go to work in the factories. It showed a picture of a strong woman who worked on an assembly line. Her name was Rosie the Riveter. She told the person reading the poster, "We can do it!" This meant that women could work just as well as men.

The poster worked really well. Soon, women all over the country took over for men in the factories. They used heavy machinery and worked many long hours on assembly lines. They built tanks, airplanes, and other vehicles.

Without these women, we probably would not have won the war. When it was all over, many women went back to their homes. Others kept their jobs and continued working. They helped change a lot of minds in a short time. People began to realize that women were just as skilled as men.

Today, things are different. Men and women work side by side in nearly every kind of job. Rosie the Riveter's message is still true. We can do it, together.

Go On

Book 1

6 Read the chart below.

Jobs Most Women Did Before World War II
They were homemakers.
They worked in hospitals as nurses.
?

Which sentence **best** completes the chart?

A They taught children.

B They joined the army.

C They worked in factories.

D They worked for the government.

7 The government solved the problem of how to keep making airplanes and other vehicles when they

A thought women were not as good workers as men

B got many men to join the armed forces to help win the war

C made a poster that encouraged women to work in factories

D asked all nurses and teachers to start working on assembly lines

8 According to the article, how were men and women alike in the 1940s?

A They both worked well in factories.

B They both went off to fight in a war.

C They both worked mainly as homemakers.

D They both did mostly nursing or teaching jobs.

9 Read these sentences from the article.

> **At this time, most women were homemakers. If a woman had a job outside of the home, it was usually a job held mostly by women, such as nurse or teacher.**

What does the word "homemakers" **most likely** mean?

A people who build homes

B people who work in the home

C people who do not work at all

D people who do work as nurses or teachers

10 What is this article **mostly** about?

A how men decided to work in the home

B how the United States won World War II

C how the Rosie the Riveter poster was made

D how women started working in new kinds of jobs

11 According to the article, which statement is **true**?

A Women were not skilled at factory work.

B Women used to work mostly as homemakers.

C Women did not want to help the war effort.

D Women did not like the Rosie the Riveter poster.

Go On

12 After reading the article, what could the reader conclude?

A Women mainly do the jobs that men cannot do.

B Men do not really work on assembly lines anymore.

C Women have more work opportunities now than they once did.

D Airplane factories were the most important part of winning the war.

13 Which of these details is **most** important to the article?

A how Rosie the Riveter looked

B what supplies factories could make

C who created the Rosie the Riveter poster

D why women began working in the factories

Book 1

Directions

Read this poem. Then answer questions 14 through 17.

The Fieldmouse

by Cecil Frances Alexander

Where the acorn tumbles down,
    Where the ash tree sheds its berry,
With your fur so soft and brown,
    With your eye so round and merry,
Scarcely moving the long grass,
Fieldmouse, I can see you pass.

Little thing, in what dark den,
    Lie you all the winter sleeping
Till warm weather comes again?
    Then once more I see you peeping
Round about the tall tree roots,
Nibbling at their fallen fruits.

Fieldmouse, fieldmouse, do not go,
    Where the farmer stacks his treasure,
Find the nut that falls below,
    Eat the acorn at your pleasure,
But you must not steal the grain
He has stacked with so much pain.

Make your hole where mosses spring,
    Underneath the tall oak's shadow,
Pretty, quiet harmless thing,
    Play about the sunny meadow,
Keep away from corn and house,
None will harm you, little mouse.

Go On

14 Which statement **best** describes the mouse in the poem?

    A The mouse is small and cute.

    B The mouse likes to climb trees.

    C The mouse has to eat a lot of food.

    D The mouse is sneaky and naughty.

15 Why does the mouse stay in a dark den?

    A It hides all its food there.

    B It lives there in the spring.

    C It sleeps there through the winter.

    D It must hide its food from the farmer.

16 What does the poet compare to a treasure?

    A the warm weather

    B the farmer's grains

    C the mouse's acorns

    D the sunny meadow

17 Why does the poet **most likely** include the warning about the corn and house?

    A to tempt the mouse to look for these forbidden things

    B to show that the farmer will not take the mouse's acorns

    C to explain why mice get sick when they eat people's food

    D to prevent the mouse from doing harm and being harmed

Directions
Read this story. Then answer questions 18 through 22.

A Hula from Hawaii

by Lydia Yi

Linda Simpson stared out of the kitchen window. It was a beautiful day. The sun was shining and only a few white clouds drifted across the blue sky. She never saw any of it though. Linda was too busy worrying.

"Isn't it lovely today?" asked Mrs. Simpson. "Linda? Hello, Mother to Linda. Are you in there?"

With a start, Linda turned around and saw her mother. One look at her daughter's face and Mrs. Simpson knew something was wrong.

"Are you still worrying about your school project?" she asked.

Linda nodded. "I have to tell my teacher tomorrow what kind of demonstration I am going to give about Hawaii. I still don't have any ideas about the kind of project I want to do. It seems like all of the other kids have really cool or really exciting ideas. Alex and Brendan are making a volcano that actually erupts. Alanna is bringing in food that she is making from her grandmother's favorite Hawaiian recipes. Jasmine is presenting different Hawaiian shirt designs. What can I do that would be just as much fun? I'm doomed!"

Just then, her younger brother Kevin came through the door. "Mom," he shouted, "Mr. and Mrs. Connors are back from their vacation. Come see what they brought us."

Mrs. Simpson patted her daughter on the arm and then went into the front yard to welcome her neighbors back home. They had just returned from two weeks in Hawaii!

"Hey," thought Mrs. Simpson, as an idea came out of the blue. "Maybe they can help Linda."

Go On

A few minutes later, Linda found herself in the Connors' living room. Her mother had found the perfect solution. Mrs. Connors had learned how to hula dance while she was in Hawaii, and she was going to teach Linda.

Mrs. Connors gave Linda a grass skirt to wear. She turned on some Hawaiian music and began moving her hips and her hands. Mrs. Connors asked Linda to come stand next to her. She showed Linda how to move her hands like slow rolling waves in the ocean.

"I always thought that hula dancers told a story with their hands," said Mrs. Connors. "But only part of the message is told with hand movement. The rest is told with words as you dance."

Linda grinned with excitement. This was going to be a fun lesson. It was going to be even more fun to show it off in school!

---

18 Which event happens **first** in the story?

   A Kevin comes into the kitchen.

   B Mrs. Connors gives Linda a grass skirt.

   C Linda moves her hands like rolling ocean waves.

   D Mrs. Simpson has a good idea for Linda's project.

19 What is the **main** problem in the story?

   A Linda wants to take a vacation to Hawaii.

   B Mrs. Simpson cannot get her daughter's attention.

   C Linda cannot think of an idea for her school project.

   D Mrs. Connors must teach Linda how to do a hula dance.

    Book 1

20 Why do the neighbors in the story know how to help Linda?

    A They have gifts for her.

    B They were just in Hawaii.

    C They are teachers at her school.

    D They know a lot about everything.

21 Here is a web about the story.

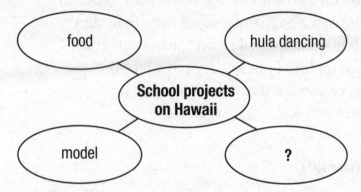

Which phrase **best** completes this web?

    A history of Hawaii

    B wildlife of Hawaii

    C Hawaiian shirt designs

    D Hawaiian myths and legends

22 Which sentence from the story **best** describes Linda's attitude about hula dancing?

    A "Linda was too busy worrying."

    B "They had just returned from two weeks in Hawaii!"

    C "Mrs. Connors gave Linda a grass skirt to wear."

    D "Linda grinned with excitement."

Go On

Directions
Read this article. Then answer questions 23 through 28.

A Winter Tradition

by Emilio Vargas

Many families carry on a special tradition every snowy winter. First, they roll the snow into three balls. They make a large ball, a medium-sized ball, and a small ball. Then they stack the balls. The largest ball is placed on the bottom and the smallest ball is put on top. Finally, they put a face on the smallest ball, and clothe the stack of snow. They have completed their snowman!

History of the Snowman

The very first snowman was made right here in the United States. It was invented in Eau Claire, Wisconsin, during the winter of 1809. A man named Vernon Paul was playing in the snow with his nine-year-old daughter. He told her they needed to frighten away elves who try to steal holiday presents. So, they built a snowman to scare the elves. The snowman was kind of like a scarecrow that scares away birds. Soon, everyone in town built one of their own. Before long, people were building snowmen all over the country and the world!

The World's Biggest Snowman

The largest snowman ever built was over 113 feet tall! It was made in Bethel, Maine, in the winter of 1999. It took nine million pounds of snow to make it. Four-foot wreathes were used for its eyes. Six feet of wire and cloth formed its carrot-like nose. Its mouth and buttons were made up of car tires. The snowman also had a 20-foot hat, and a 120-foot scarf. Ten-foot trees were used for its arms! The enormous snowman melted in June of 1999.

Making Your Own Snowman

Making a snowman can be a lot of fun. But what if you do not have any snow? No problem! Follow these steps to make your own snowman at any time of year.

Book 1

Materials

- three paper sacks (each should be a different size)
- newspaper
- glue
- piece of cardboard (12 inches by 12 inches)
- aluminum foil
- tape
- 1-pound box of powdered laundry detergent (white)
- water
- paints

Tools

- spoon
- paintbrush

What to Do

1. Fill the three sacks with wads of newspaper. Fold the sacks to form them into balls. Then, glue the three balls to form a snowman. The largest ball goes on the bottom, and the smallest goes on the top. Let the glue dry while you cover the cardboard with foil and glue it in place.

2. Next, glue the snowman shape to the foil-covered cardboard. Mix the laundry detergent with enough water to make a thick paste. Use the spoon to spread the paste over the snowman shape. Cover it completely, smooth out the paste, and let the soapy snowman dry.

3. Finally, use paint to make the eyes, nose, and mouth. On the sides of the snowman, paint the outlines of arms with hands colored so they look like mittens. Some paint may be absorbed by detergent that is not yet dry. Repaint the features as necessary.

4. If you wish, you can add a hat and a small scarf to your figure. To display, place your snowman in a window or on a table.

---

23 What should you do **right before** gluing the three balls together?

  A Fold the sacks to form balls.
  B Fill the sacks with newspaper.
  C Cover the cardboard with foil.
  D Mix laundry detergent and water.

Go On

24 What information can be found in the section "History of the Snowman"?

    A the way to make your own snowman

    B the size of the largest snowman ever

    C the story of the snowman's invention

    D the reason snowmen have carrot noses

25 In which step of "What to Do" do you use a spoon?

    A step 1

    B step 2

    C step 3

    D step 4

26 What should you do **right after** covering the snowman shape with paste?

    A Let the paste dry.

    B Smooth out the paste.

    C Glue foil to the cardboard.

    D Paint a face on the snowman.

27 According to the article, why was the first snowman made?

    A to follow tradition

    B to frighten away birds

    C to play a joke on someone

    D to scare away thieving elves

28 The author **most likely** wrote "Making Your Own Snowman" in order to

    A teach readers about the history of snowmen

    B explain the importance of traditions

    C share ideas about a fun winter project

    D entertain readers with a story about snowmen

STOP

New York State, Empire Edition, English Language Arts, Grade 4

POSTTEST
Book 2

Name: _____

TIPS FOR TAKING THE TEST

Here are some suggestions to help you do your best:

- Be sure to read carefully all the directions in the test book.
- Plan your time.
- Read each question carefully and think about the answer before writing your response.

In this test, you will be writing about texts that you will be listening to or reading. Your writing will be scored on

- how clearly you organize your writing and express what you have learned
- how accurately and completely you answer the questions being asked
- how well you support your responses with examples of details from the text
- how correctly you use grammar, spelling, punctuation, capitalization, and paragraphing

Listening and Writing

Directions

In this part of the test, you are going to listen to a story called "The Silver on the Hearth." Then you will answer questions 29 through 31 about the story.

You will listen to the story twice. The first time you hear the story, listen carefully but do not take notes. As you listen to the story the second time, you may want to take notes. Use the space below and on the next page for your notes. You may use these notes to answer the questions that follow. Your notes on these pages will NOT count toward your final score.

Notes

Notes

Go On

29 The chart below shows what happens in the story. Complete the chart with details from the story.

WHAT HAPPENS IN THIS STORY

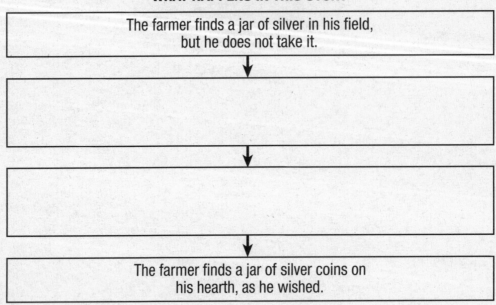

The farmer finds a jar of silver in his field, but he does not take it.

↓

↓

↓

The farmer finds a jar of silver coins on his hearth, as he wished.

30 In the story, how does seeing the jar of silver coins on his hearth change the farmer's way of thinking about the jar? Use details from the story to support your answer.

_____

_____

_____

_____

_____

You may plan your writing for question 31 on a separate sheet of paper.

31

The farmer's feelings change in the story. How does he feel at the **beginning** of the story? How does he feel at the **end** of the story? What causes his feelings to change? Use details from the story to support your answer.

In your answer, be sure to include

- how the farmer feels at the **beginning** of the story
- how the farmer feels at the **end** of the story
- what causes the farmer's feelings to change
- details from the story to support your answer

Check your writing for correct spelling, grammar, capitalization, and punctuation.

Go On

STOP

New York State, Empire Edition, English Language Arts, Grade 4

POSTTEST
Book 3

Name: _____

TIPS FOR TAKING THE TEST

Here are some suggestions to help you do your best:

- Be sure to read carefully all the directions in the test book.
- Plan your time.
- Read each question carefully and think about the answer before writing your response.

In this test, you will be writing about texts that you will be listening to or reading. Your writing will be scored on

- how clearly you organize your writing and express what you have learned
- how accurately and completely you answer the questions being asked
- how well you support your responses with examples of details from the text
- how correctly you use grammar, spelling, punctuation, capitalization, and paragraphing

Reading and Writing

Directions

In this part of the test, you are going to read a story called "Why Spiders Have Thin Waists" and a passage called "Eight-Legged Wonders." You will answer questions 32 through 35 and write about what you have read. You may look back at the story and passage as often as you like.

Why Spiders Have Thin Waists

a West African folktale

Anansi the spider loved to dance. He loved to take naps under a shady tree. But most of all, he loved to eat.

One day, he was awakened from a nap by his older brother. Older Brother told Anansi that they were invited to a wedding on the next day, north of their village. Anansi knew that a wedding also meant a wedding feast. There would be dancing and there would be all kinds of delicious food. His mouth began to water at the very thought of it.

After Older Brother went on his way, Anansi went back to his nap. He wanted to be certain he had a good rest so he could dance the next day. As he slept, he dreamed about all the wonderful food there would be at the feast.

Just as he was eating cake in his dream, his younger brother awakened him. Younger Brother told Anansi they were invited to a wedding on the next day, south of the village. Anansi couldn't believe his luck. Two wedding feasts on the same day—he needed a plan so he could attend both weddings! He then decided that he should take a long nap so he would be rested for all the thinking he needed to do.

The next morning, Older Brother arrived. Anansi told Older Brother that he should go ahead to the wedding. Anansi tied a rope around his waist and told Older Brother to pull on the rope when the wedding began. Anansi would then go north to the wedding feast. With eight legs, a spider can walk quickly. Older Brother went on his way with the rope.

When Younger Brother arrived, Anansi told him that he should go ahead to the wedding. Anansi tied another rope around his waist and told Younger Brother to pull on the rope when the wedding began. Anansi would then go south to the wedding feast. Younger Brother agreed and went on his way south, holding firmly to the end of the rope. He then settled down under the shady tree to take a small nap, knowing that whoever tugged on the rope would wake him.

Anansi woke with a start. Older Brother was tugging at the rope from the north. Anansi was just about to head north when Younger Brother tugged on his rope from the south. Anansi couldn't move—his brothers were pulling him in opposite directions.

Older Brother didn't know why Anansi wasn't running north, so he pulled harder on his rope. Younger Brother knew Anansi would be angry if he missed the feast, so he pulled harder on his rope. Anansi couldn't untie the ropes from his waist—and his waist was getting thinner and thinner. Finally, his brothers gave up and a very tired Anansi with a very thin waist fell asleep.

Ever since that day, all spiders have thin waists to remind them of Anansi, so they will not follow his example.

---

32 In the story, what is the problem that Anansi faces? How does he decide to solve the problem? Use details from the story to support your answer.

_____

_____

_____

_____

_____

Go On

Eight-Legged Wonders

by Beth Chang

Spiders are truly remarkable creatures. These insects have eight legs, and up to eight eyes! Their bodies are divided into two main parts. These parts are connected by a narrow stalk. This special body design allows spiders to twist in many different directions. Spiders come in almost every color imaginable. There are dull gray and brown spiders, and black or white ones. There are even bright red, yellow, orange, green, or blue spiders.

The most amazing thing about a spider is its ability to make silk. Spider silk looks delicate, but it is actually a very strong material. It is very difficult to break because it stretches so easily. A spider's silk can also be very sticky. It is used to make nests and sacs for eggs. Some spiders use it like a parachute to slow a fall or travel on the wind. Many spiders also use their silken threads to create beautiful webs. This is how some spiders get their food.

Spider webs are made to trap other insects like flies, bees, and moths. The insects get tangled in the sticky threads of the web. Once the insect is caught up in the web, the spider may wrap it in more silk. The spider may also use its fangs to bite the insect. Most spiders shoot out venom, or poison, through their fangs. This may kill the trapped insect. Or, it makes it impossible for the insect to move.

Not all spiders capture their meals with webs, though. Many spiders hunt for their food. For example, jumping spiders and ground spiders may hide in tiny holes. Their body color and shape help them blend in with their surroundings. When a tasty insect comes near, the spider leaps onto it. Again, the spider uses its fangs and venom to finish off the insect.

The venom of most spiders is not dangerous to humans. In fact, most kinds of spider are so small that their fangs cannot break human skin. However, there are a few types of spiders that can pose a threat to people. But even these cannot usually kill healthy adults.

There is only one common type of spider in New York that can be poisonous to people. That is the Northern Black Widow. These spiders have a very unusual color pattern. They are shiny black with diagonal white stripes on their sides. They also have red dots running down the top of their bodies and a bright-red mark on their underside. This mark may look a bit like an hourglass. Like most spiders, Northern Black Widows will not usually attack people. The spiders only bite if they feel that they must defend themselves or their eggs.

33 Spiders share many common features, but different kinds of spiders can have different traits and behaviors. Give **two** ways that spiders are different from one another. Use details from the passage in your answer.

1. _____

   _____

   _____

2. _____

   _____

   _____

Go On

34 Complete the chart below with three details from the passage that show how spiders use their silk.

How Spiders Use Their Silk
1)
2)
3)

Planning Page

You may PLAN your writing for question 35 here if you wish, but do NOT write your final answer on this page. Your writing on this Planning Page will not count toward your final score. Write your final answer on Pages 258 and 259.

Answer

Go On

The story "Why Spiders Have Thin Waists" describes a feature of spiders. Why did spiders get this feature according to the story? Now think about how that feature is described in the passage "Eight Legged Wonders." What reasons are given for the feature in this passage? Tell how the reasons given in the passage and story are **different**. Use details from **both** the story and the passage to support your answer.

In your answer, be sure to

- tell what feature is described in the story
- explain why spiders have this feature according to the story
- tell how that feature is described in the passage
- name the **different** reason the passage gives for the feature
- use details from **both** the story and the passage to support your answer

Check your writing for correct spelling, grammar, capitalization, and punctuation.

_____

_____

_____

_____

_____

_____

_____

STOP

Notes

Notes

Notes

Notes

Notes